© 2019 by Miguel Gonçalves

No rights reserved. Any part of this book may be reproduced, stored in a retrieval system, or transmitted by any means, electronic, mechanical, photocopying, recording, or otherwise, without prior permission of the publisher.

Published by Portokalia
apophthegm.portokalia.co.uk

ISBN: 978-1-58435-050-3
Distributed by Miguel Gonçalves
Printed in the United Kingdom
10 9 8 7 6 5

# APOPHTHEGM

If you were as honest as I am,
you would be writing the same book as me.

# Contents

| | | |
|---|---|---|
| I. | Iconoclast | 9 |
| II. | SAMO© | 15 |
| III. | Fetish | 27 |
| IV. | Electability | 43 |
| V. | Cogency | 63 |
| VI. | Hegemony | 73 |
| VII. | Value | 89 |
| VIII. | Hysteria | 101 |
| IX. | Class | 109 |
| X. | Laika | 121 |
| XI. | Tourism | 143 |
| XII. | Past | 173 |
| XIII. | Kispo | 187 |

# I
# Iconoclast

### Example

Picture me ascending a very high, steep and hitherto unexplored mountain. Assume that I have overcome unprecedented difficulties and dangers and I have succeeded in reaching a much higher point than any of my predecessors, but I have still not reached the summit. I would find myself in a position where it is not only difficult and dangerous to proceed in the direction and along the path I have chosen, but positively impossible. I am forced to turn back, descend, seek another path, longer, perhaps, but one that will enable me to reach the summit. The descent from the height that no one before me have reached proves to be more dangerous and difficult than the ascent — it is easier to slip; it is not so easy to choose a foothold; there is not that exhilaration that one feels in going upwards, straight to the goal. I have to tie a rope round myself, spend hours with all alpenstock to cut footholds or a projection to which the rope could be tied firmly; I have to move at a snail's pace, and move downwards, descend, away from the goal; and I do not know where this extremely dangerous and painful descent will end, or whether there is a fairly safe detour by which I can ascend more boldly, more quickly and more directly to the summit.

It would hardly be natural to suppose that given the unprecedented height climbed I did not have his moments of despondency. These moments were more numerous, more frequent and harder to bear if I

## APOPHTHEGM

heard the voices of those below, who, through a telescope and from a safe distance, are watching my dangerous descent, which cannot even be described as ascending with the brakes on; brakes presuppose a well designed and tested vehicle, a well-prepared road and previously tested appliances. In this case, however, there is no vehicle, no road, absolutely nothing that had been tested beforehand.

The voices from below ring with malicious joy. They do not conceal it; they chuckle gleefully and shout: "He'll fall in a minute! Serve him right, the lunatic!" Others try to conceal their malicious glee. They moan and raise their eyes to heaven in sorrow, as if to say: "It grieves us sorely to see our fears justified! But did not we, who have spent all our lives working out a judicious plan for scaling this mountain, demand that the ascent be postponed until our plan was complete? And if we so vehemently protested against taking this path, which this lunatic is now abandoning (look, look, he has turned back! He is descending! A single step is taking him hours of preparation! And yet we were roundly abused when time and again we demanded moderation and caution!), if we so fervently censured this lunatic and warned everybody against imitating and helping him, we did so entirely because of our devotion to the great plan to scale this mountain, and in order to prevent this great plan from being generally discredited!"

Luckily, I cannot hear the voices of these people who are true friends of the idea of ascent; if I did, they would probably nauseate me. And nausea does not help one to keep a clear head and a firm step, particularly at high altitudes.

### Everyone else is sick of Miguel Gonçalves, but I can't get enough of him

I am an honest man who does not always tell the truth.

I hunt down the obvious with the enthusiasm of a short-sighted detective.

I am a member of the *Club dei Brutti* where ugliness is a virtue, beauty is slavery.

# ICONOCLAST

I know where I came from, but where did all you zombies come from?

I don't have to be working class to be in the side of the working class.

I spend more time critiquing the Left than the Right because it is the Left I am trying to organise.

I believe revolutionary bloodshed is both necessary and defensible.

I would have loved to dance in the snow outside the Winter Palace to celebrate the seventy-third day of Soviet power — the lifespan of the Commune plus one.

My idols are dead and my enemies are in power.

I adapt the moral rule of my condition, but I never compromise about the dogma on which it rests.

I resist evil by resisting the seductive force of surface appearances and conventional things.

The imperfect is my only paradise.

It is not clear to me that the past actually gives us any lessons.

One day I will renounce free choice and live according to the dictation of dice.

I am the visible proof that idealism is no figment of the imagination, but the truth.

I consume to perform an idea of myself.

I am one of god's prototypes — a high powered mutant never considered for mass production. Too weird to live and too rare to die.

My life may be sad, but it's always beautiful.

## Sometimes I feel I am explaining cigarettes to a robot

Making sense of the world is for a thinker who is deeper and better organised than I.

# APOPHTHEGM

I am here mostly to be misunderstood.

Praise me less and understand me more.

I long to confuse things.

Talking to people unlike myself is hard.

I am the barbarian, because I am not understood by anyone.

I am a genuinely original mind, which does typically exhibit, not randomly but intelligibly, significant structural contradictions.

I still believe there can be moments in history when everything might be turned upside down once again. But today I have to declare myself defeatist.

If my arguments are attacked by everyone, then this is a reliable sign that I am in the right.

I am not interested in providing solutions to problems. I often ask questions not necessarily in search of answers as much as in an effort to try to determine the lens through which one must view the problem in order to hypothetically solve it.

I can break an awful lot of eggs without making a decent omelette.

One can be right and yet be beaten, force can vanquish spirit, and there are times when courage is not rewarded.

My homesickness is for a home that had been so radically altered that it no longer really exists.

## I am an exophonic writer

The recording of my inner life is becoming an unintentional parody of my inner life.

It is only shallow people who do not judge by appearances. The mystery of the world is the visible, not the invisible.

I didn't lose all this weight for body positivity to become a thing.

I dismiss those unfamiliar with chrestomathy as ignoramuses and suggest that everyone leave my vocabulary and me to my own customers, who have all been to school.

A lexicon is closer to a chrestomathy — of words and idioms, obviously, but of morphemes, too, when necessary.

I threw a party for time travellers — invitations sent only after the fact: I sat there a long time, but no one came.

I am proud of scars on my body. They are an autograph signed to me by a world grateful for my continued willingness to play with it, even when I don't feel like it.

I established a theoretical model of thought. How could I have suspected that people would want to implement it with Molotov cocktails?

I act in ways that could be generalised to universal principles.

I bring together things that have never been brought together and do not seem predisposed to be so.

Things could be as they should be or things are as they have to be.

My work consists of two parts: the one presented here plus all that I have not written. And, it is precisely this second part that is the important one.

# II
# SAMO©

## Futurism

We want to sing the love of danger, the habit of energy and rashness.

The essential elements of our poetry will be courage, audacity and revolt.

Literature has up to now magnified pensive immobility, ecstasy and slumber. We want to exalt movements of aggression, feverish sleeplessness, the double march, the perilous leap, the slap and the blow with the fist.

We declare that the splendour of the world has been enriched by a new beauty: the beauty of speed. A racing automobile with its bonnet adorned with great tubes like serpents with explosive breath, a roaring motor car which seems to run on machine-gun fire, is more beautiful than the Victory of Samothrace.

We want to sing the man at the wheel, the ideal axis of which crosses the earth, itself hurled along its orbit.

The poet must spend himself with warmth, glamour and prodigality to increase the enthusiastic fervour of the primordial elements.

Beauty exists only in struggle. There is no masterpiece that has not an aggressive character. Poetry must be a violent assault on the forces of the unknown, to force them to bow before man.

# APOPHTHEGM

We are on the extreme promontory of the centuries! What is the use of looking behind at the moment when we must open the mysterious shutters of the impossible? Time and Space died yesterday. We are already living in the absolute, since we have already created eternal, omnipresent speed.

We want to glorify war — the only cure for the world — militarism, patriotism, the destructive gesture of the anarchists, the beautiful ideas which kill, and contempt for woman.

We want to demolish museums and libraries, fight morality, feminism and all opportunist and utilitarian cowardice.

We will sing of the great crowds agitated by work, pleasure and revolt; the multi-coloured and polyphonic surf of revolutions in modern capitals: the nocturnal vibration of the arsenals and the workshops beneath their violent electric moons: the gluttonous railway stations devouring smoking serpents; factories suspended from the clouds by the thread of their smoke; bridges with the leap of gymnasts flung across the diabolic cutlery of sunny rivers: adventurous steamers sniffing the horizon; great-breasted locomotives, puffing on the rails like enormous steel horses with long tubes for bridle, and the gliding flight of aeroplanes whose propeller sounds like the flapping of a flag and the applause of enthusiastic crowds.

It is in Italy that we are issuing this manifesto of ruinous and incendiary violence, by which we today are founding Futurism, because we want to deliver Italy from its gangrene of professors, archaeologists, tourist guides and antiquaries.

Italy has been too long the great second-hand market. We want to get rid of the innumerable museums which cover it with innumerable cemeteries.

Museums, cemeteries! Truly identical in their sinister juxtaposition of bodies that do not know each other. Public dormitories where you sleep side by side for ever with beings you hate or do not know. Reciprocal ferocity of the painters and sculptors who murder each other in the same museum with blows of line and color. To make a visit once a year, as one goes to see the graves of our dead once a year, that we could allow! We can even imagine placing flowers once a year at the feet of the Gioconda! But to take our sadness, our fragile courage and our anxiety to the museum every day, that we cannot admit! Do you want to poison yourselves? Do you want to rot?

What can you find in an old picture except the painful contortions of the artist trying to break uncrossable barriers which obstruct the full expression of his dream?

To admire an old picture is to pour our sensibility into a funeral urn instead of casting it forward with violent spurts of creation and action. Do you want to waste the best part of your strength in a useless admiration of the past, from which you will emerge exhausted, diminished, trampled on?

Indeed daily visits to museums, libraries and academies (those cemeteries of wasted effort, calvaries of crucified dreams, registers of false starts!) is for artists what prolonged supervision by the parents is for intelligent young men, drunk with their own talent and ambition.

For the dying, for invalids and for prisoners it may be all right. It is, perhaps, some sort of balm for their wounds, the admirable past, at a moment when the future is denied them. But we will have none of it, we, the young, strong and living Futurists!

Let the good incendiaries with charred fingers come! Here they are! Heap up the fire to the shelves of the libraries! Divert the canals to flood the cellars of the museums! Let the glorious canvases swim ashore! Take the picks and hammers! Undermine the foundation of venerable towns!

The oldest among us are not yet thirty years old: we have therefore at least ten years to accomplish our task. When we are forty let younger and stronger men than we throw us in the waste paper basket like useless manuscripts! They will come against us from afar, leaping on the light cadence of their first poems, clutching the air with their predatory fingers and sniffing at the gates of the academies the good scent of our decaying spirits, already promised to the catacombs of the

# APOPHTHEGM

libraries.

But we shall not be there. They will find us at last one winter's night in the depths of the country in a sad hangar echoing with the notes of the monotonous rain, crouched near our trembling aeroplanes, warming our hands at the wretched fire which our books of today will make when they flame gaily beneath the glittering flight of their pictures.

They will crowd around us, panting with anguish and disappointment, and exasperated by our proud indefatigable courage, will hurl themselves forward to kill us, with all the more hatred as their hearts will be drunk with love and admiration for us. And strong healthy Injustice will shine radiantly from their eyes. For art can only be violence, cruelty, injustice.

The oldest among us are not yet thirty, and yet we have already wasted treasures, treasures of strength, love, courage and keen will, hastily, deliriously, without thinking, with all our might, till we are out of breath.

Look at us! We are not out of breath, our hearts are not in the least tired. For they are nourished by fire, hatred and speed! Does this surprise you? it is because you do not even remember being alive! Standing on the world's summit, we launch once more our challenge to the stars!

Your objections? All right! I know them! Of course! We know just what our beautiful false intelligence affirms: "We are only the sum and the prolongation of our ancestors," it says. Perhaps! All right! What does it matter? But we will not listen! Take care not to repeat those infamous words! Instead, lift up your head!

Standing on the world's summit we launch once again our insolent challenge to the stars!

## Something repeated ten times is the opposite of art

Culture is the norm, art is the exception.

Authenticity in art is only an aesthetic effect.

The thing about "Never sell out!" is that it sells.

Art has its premonitions, though they are not always right.

Is the purpose of art to criticise life or to be an extension of life?

It is not the duty of intellectuals to be reassuring and edifying, to create a serious world for adult children to wrap themselves up in: they are supposed to be critics not clerics.

The world doesn't change, what changes is art.

Self-created roles become as constraining as the social roles from which they are meant to provide ironic detachment. We long for the suspension of self-consciousness, of the pseudoanalytic attitude that has become second nature; but neither art nor religion, historically the great emancipators from the prison of the self, retain the power to discourage disbelief.

From a bourgeois point of view it is impossible to conceive a history of art which is not Christian and Roman Catholic.

Art collecting is the most esteemed form of shopping in our culture today.

The artwork behaves much like a luxury commodity, the cost of which is deducted from profits rather than from wages.

Instagram shows us what a world without art looks like.

From friendship comes creativity.

Contemporary art has the feature that the arts itself adopts the critique the art is going to get.

Follow the rule about how to break the rules, and you'll be guaranteed success.

The aura of an original work of art arises only after, and not before, it is copied.

Today we have creators making content rather than artists making art.

Abstraction encourages action, as remembrance leads to innovation.

When the *Mona Lisa* was stolen from the Louvre in 1911 more people visited the museum to see the empty space than had ever come to see the painting.

Artists have shunned the machine because human greed has usurped it and made it a terrible engine of enslavement, deluging the world with murderous ubiquity, which was plainly enough the damnation of their art and craft.

A professional caste of artists and intellectuals becomes possible only when not everyone needs to labour for most of the time.

Goldman Sachs has been depicted as the central villain of the Great Recession. Yet little has been said about its most egregious sin: the lobby art.

## Culture is the opium of the intelligentsia

It's not hard to formulate the trends for our times: SoulCycle, green juice, butter coffee, tarot, ayahuasca, group retreats to the Omega Institute, hypnotism to quit smoking, The Secret, antivaccination, polyphasic sleep, Burning Man, kale.

Authentic goods are produced through the manipulation of social context, rather than some purification process.

Our economy is our culture and our culture is for sale.

The fate of the Chelsea Manning, Edward Snowden and Julian Assange are high-profile advertisements for a culture of, while abusing authority may be bad, openly pointing out that someone is abusing authority is much worse and merits the severest punishment.

In a remarkable historical irony, the political victory of humanism spelled the cultural defeat of the humanities.

To gain meaning is a cultural accomplishment, not technical one.

All cultures and identities can be understood, provided that one makes an effort to get it.

Millennials have the best TV, even if Generation X had the best music.

The cultural class, formerly known as hipsters, now exercises a full monopoly on the meaning of millennial.

Our culture operates on that ludicrous adage comparing sex to pizza. Even when it's bad, it's still pretty good.

The odds of a meme going viral are comparable to winning the lottery, but the lottery actually pays out in cash.

The cultural politics of transgression, so long fetishised by the left, have been triumphantly adopted by the right.

Pop culture is intrinsically fascist, and nerd culture especially so.

Pseudo-events such as the European Capital of Culture are further catalysts for the city's transformation into a commodity.

Hamilton has been called the cultural event of our time, however, it is a corporate HR department's wet dream that is totally unknown to nearly all who actually live in our time.

Disneyfication used to mean sanitisation and infantilisation. Now, Disney comes to represent nothing less than the smooth functioning of media capitalism.

## Without critical comparison, reading is intellectually and aesthetically blind

Writing collectivises individual memory; reading individualises collective memory.

Language makes infinite use of finite means.

Any new term is jargon before it becomes a new term.

Word meanings must always pass through the mind of language users in a way that is highly context- and goal-dependent.

The book creates meaning, the meaning creates life.

Too long; didn't read (abbreviated tl;dr and tldr) is a shorthand notation added by an editor indicating a passage appeared to be too long to invest the time to digest.

A writer venturing into the wild with a smartphone and a notepad has got to be joking; only scientists and civil servants should be doing this.

It is quite unnatural that the writer should write all the time and in all situations. The opposite treats literary production as a sort of involuntary secretion, which is taboo, since it escapes human determinations: to speak more decorously, the writer is prey of an inner god who speaks at all times, without bothering, tyrant that he is, with the holidays of this medium. Writers are holiday, but their muse is awake, and gives birth non-stop.

Angela Nagle's *Kill All Normies* is guaranteed to transform any leftist get together into a struggle session.

Naomi Klein is the Malcolm Gladwell of the left.

Norman Mailer briefly shared a jail cell with Noam Chomsky.

John Steinbeck was a bad husband. How bad? On his wedding night, he spent more than an hour on the phone with his mistress.

Voltaire made the parable a vehicle for the ideas that would shatter the 18th century.

It is Proust's courtesy to spare the reader the embarrassment of believing himself cleverer than the author.

*Hamlet* and *Don Quixote* represent the opposite extremes of human nature, if not of nature itself. Together they define the fundamental forces of all that exists. They explain the growth of flowers to us, and they even enable us to comprehend the development of the most powerful nations. *Hamlet* incarnates inertia, *Don Quixote* progress. Shakespeare's brooding hero proves relentlessly ironic, rational, and perceptive, but cannot act. Believing in nothing but his own judgment, he grows completely self-absorbed and unable to love. *Don Quixote* is just the reverse, all will and no sense. The man of faith, he credulously accepts an ideal of goodness without suspecting he mistakes desire for fact. To his own detriment, he lives entirely selflessly, inherently incapable of betraying his convictions or transferring them from one object to another. *Hamlet* represents the aristocratic superfluous man, who was cultivated but lethargic, while *Don Quixote* recalled the idealist revolutionary, believing foolishly in an impossible, if noble, ideal.

The nine circles of hell from the inferno in *The Divine Comedy* represent the nine months that the embryo spends in the mother's womb.

Science fiction has increasingly shifted away from utopian imaginings, and is now either dwelling on the wonders and terrors of the techno-futuristic present or forecasting inevitable apocalyptic collapse.

The trouble with fiction is that it makes too much sense. Reality never makes sense.

## The flame of cinema was extinguished for good at Auschwitz

A film has to be penetrated in order to be interpreted.

Films create a world more in accordance with our desires than with reality.

The only true criticism of a film is another film.

Difficult cinema is the most democratic, because you are doing your audience the honour of supposing that they are intelligent human beings. So much of the cinema of today treats people as if they are fools.

## APOPHTHEGM

Today's cinema is a liberated, individual cinema in which you don't know what to do.

Universities, as late as the 1930s, refused to teach writers later than the Romantics. The assumption was that no one needed to teach contemporary writers, for earnest students would eventually read them on their own, if not now then later. The same applied to movies; one doesn't need to teach or theorise about the movies — one goes to the movies.

Cinema's roots had been in science, but cinema was quickly seduced by the allure of glamour and profit to become an offshoot of the cosmetics industry.

Indie films are just a market segment for big studios.

Any completist film historian is on a one-way road to the asylum.

Instead of identifying with the characters the audience should be astonished at the circumstances under which they function.

The audience doesn't know what they want. If they did, they wouldn't be the fucking audience.

Applause is the echo of a platitude.

*Avatar 2* and *3* are James Cameron *Chinese Democracy*.

I generally can't sustain any thoughts about Richard Linklater work. I only retain a general sense of having periodically wasted hours of my life that I'm never getting back.

The face of Garbo is an idea, that of Hepburn, an event.

Carla Bruni looked like a first lady might look in a Hollywood film about a first lady.

One thing is certain: Alejandro González Iñárritu has finally solved the problem of how to film a realistic bear fight. The next cinematic problem he should tackle is screenwriting.

*Mad Max: Fury Road* is that one-in-a-thousand reboot that will green-light even more reboots, none of which will justify its existence like this one.

The central message of *Suicide Squad* is something that's already been relentlessly imposed on us during the 2018 United States elections; it tells us to support the lesser evil. *Suicide Squad* is the Hillary Clinton campaign.

The *Battle of Algiers* is probably the only film that has ever made middle-class audiences believe in the necessity of bombing innocent people.

*Mad Men* wasn't the great existential drama of our age, exploring the nature of identity and our Freudian urges. It was just a meandering soap.

## I just finished the recent Sandy Denny biography. I was very disappointed by it. In the end, she dies

The music industry is a misnamed industry where the ultimate purpose is to reduce the amount of music being made.

In the race to adopt new technologies, the music industry historically has finished just ahead of the Amish.

We live in an era when the least remarkable feature of a Beyoncé album is that it samples Animal Collective and the Yeah Yeah Yeahs. Thank god we can admit the assumed barriers between those artists' audiences were just foolish projections of mostly white rockists who had no legacy beyond overwhelming urge to feel special, to overrate their personal blips in history.

The name Nickelback come from the band's bassist, a Starbucks barista who often had to give customers a 'nickel back' in change.

Wolf Alice are the Evanescence of the hipsters.

The Eurovision Song Contest is not a live music show that happens to be filmed, but rather a live TV show that happens to have music.

*Der Ring des Nibelungen* by Richard Wagner is a story of the gods for people who have no gods to believe in.

Philip Glass' operas say die, die, die, fools, but first give me £135 for a seat to hear me tell it.

## The house is a machine for living in

Architecture is one of the few remaining arts in which the great auteurs still exist.

Creative freedom for the architect does not result in a parallel freedom for the visitor.

There is a confusion at the heart of contemporary architecture — the difference between a window and a wall.

The ideal of housing for those on low-incomes with a degree of spaciousness and style has been lost.

There is no lack of housing, only a lack of money in the hands of workers to buy them.

In every city in the world there is an elite obsessed with inscribing its domination on the landscape in vertical form.

Gentrification is a process that hides the apparatus of domination from the dominant themselves.

Historic building preservation is effectively misguided slum appreciation.

The famous headquarters of the French Communist Party, that Oscar Niemeyer built for it, in Place Colonel Fabien was hired out to Prada for a fashion show.

# III
# Fetish

### Eligible-bachelor paradox

Women are always looking for the man who fits all the criteria. When they don't find him, they throw up their hands and settle for the sociable but unattractive, the attractive but unsociable, and, as a last resort, for the merely available.

The shortage of appealing men is a society melodrama. The shortage becomes evident as women hit their late 20s and more acute as they wander into the 30s. Some men explain their social fortune by believing they've become more attractive with age; many women prefer the far likelier explanation that male faults have become easier to overlook.

The problem of the eligible bachelor is one of the great riddles of social life. Shouldn't there be about as many highly eligible and appealing men as there are attractive, eligible women?

Actually, no — and here's why. Consider the classic version of the marriage proposal: A woman makes it known that she is open to a proposal, the man proposes, and the woman chooses to say yes or no. The structure of the proposal is not, "I choose you." It is, "Will you choose me?" A woman chooses to receive the question and chooses again once the question is asked.

The traditional concept of the search for marriage partners is like an auction. In this auction, some women will be more confident of their prospects, others less so. In game-theory terms, you would call the first group *strong bidders* and the second *weak bidders*. Your first thought might be that the *strong bidders* — women who (whether because of looks, social ability, or any other reason) are conventionally deemed more of a catch — would consistently win this kind of auction.

But this is not true. In fact, game theory suggests that auctions will often be won by *weak bidders*, who know that they can be outbid and so bid more aggressively, while the *strong bidders* will hold out for a really great deal. There is a lot at stake in getting it right in one shot, so women who are confident that they are holding a strong hand are likely to hold out and wait for the perfect prospect.

So, we arrive to the eligible-bachelor paradox. The pool of appealing men shrinks as many are married off and taken out of the game, leaving a disproportionate number of men who are notably imperfect. And, at the same time, you get a pool of women weighted toward the attractive, desirable *strong bidders*.

Where have all the most appealing men gone? Married young, and sometimes to women whose most salient characteristic was not their beauty, or passion, or intellect, but their decisiveness.

## The system is bad, but to affront it is to risk retribution

Change is inevitable; progress is optional.

We live in a world in which we can no longer imagine a better one.

The present-tense version of the world is unstable.

We obsess over fake problems while creating some real ones.

The final cataclysmic moment of destruction may never arrive. Things just go on is the catastrophe. It is not that which is approaching but that which is.

We have uncritically bought the idea that we're all one step from barbarism.

There is some confusion with the *eschatological* (what pertains to the end of the world) with the *scatological* (what pertains to excrement).

Although nature is the ultimate source of all material wealth, society applies science and technology to increase the abundance of nature; it is society and existing social relations, not nature, that limits luxury for all.

In a society where power likes to present itself in the guise of benevolence — where government seldom resorts to the naked use of force — it is hard to identify the oppressor, let alone to personify him, or to sustain a burning sense of grievance in the masses.

Our society has plenty of cash for speculation and not much for human need.

It is important to society that the public believes in free will even if learned scientists and philosophers do not.

Today's philanthropy is aimed at winning the public over to a particular ideology or viewpoint.

We want a world that is independent of our wishes yet responsive to our needs.

Glorification of splendid underdogs is nothing other than glorification of the splendid system that makes them so.

Convergence is possible only at the price of shedding identity.

Sparta is the ideal society. Small, austere, self-sufficient, fiercely patriotic, and defiantly un-cosmopolitan.

Citizenship is by its very essence less comfortable than customership.

Therapy lost the boat by internalising, coping and trying to adjust to a dysfunctional society versus seeing what its role is in changing a dysfunctional society.

Depression is an entirely rational response to the world as is. An increasingly popular response in a time of economic depression, now

## APOPHTHEGM

being dealt with by record sales of handily named anti-depressants.

A bureaucratic society that stresses cooperation, interpersonal give and take, cannot allow many legitimate outlets for anger.

In a society without authority, the lower orders no longer experience oppression as guilt. Instead, they internalise the grandiose idea of the opportunities open to all, together with an inflated opinion of their own capacities. If the lowly man resents those more highly placed, it is only because he suspects them of grandly violating the regulations of the game, as he would like to do himself if he dared. It never occurs to him to insist on a new set of rules.

The more disempowered we feel, the more we are reminded that both bad and good fortune are overwhelmingly arbitrary and out of our control, the more we are inclined to impose our own imagined patterns on the terrifying senselessness of the world.

Whether people believe in astrology or not doesn't matter as long as they absorb its messages, which uphold the system's abstract authority and divide life into day and night, work and love. The more interesting group are the half-believers who get something out of it — people who take astrology for granted, much like psychiatry, symphony concerts or political parties; they accept it because it exists, without much reflection, provided only that their own psychological demands somehow correspond to the offer. They are hardly interested in the justification of the system.

The future is always stranger than we expect: mobile phones and the Internet, not flying cars.

Concorde was seen in the sky over West London for the first time in late June 1969. Less than a month later Neil Armstrong stepped from Apollo 11 onto the moon. The future had arrived. It was tangible, it was thrilling, it was now. We came to believe that we were all part of an adventure without end. This was just the beginning, the new beginning. What we didn't realise was that this was it. A peak had been achieved. The only way was down. We would wonder what had happened to that chimera. Had it been nothing more than an evanescent abstraction? A temporal analogue of Neverland? Had Laika died in vain?

## Hipsters are people who feign an allergy to achievement to become a barista

Generation X didn't have to grow up and it is meeting a younger generation — the Millennials — that didn't have a youth.

Only the young bring anything in — and they are not young very long.

When elders make no demands on the young, they make it impossible for the young to grow up.

The fate of groups is bound up with the words that designate them.

Authenticity is, for marketers and cultural commentators, what objectivity is for scientists.

The crowd is a concept of modernity. Swarm is the new crowd.

Citizenship is the activity of co-creating a way of life.

Sometimes it feels like everyone is speaking a different language or the same language with radically different rules.

Light travels faster than sound, this is why some people appear bright until they speak.

Narcissism originates as a defence against feelings of helpless dependency in early life, which it tries to counter with blind optimism and grandiose illusions of personal self-sufficiency.

Our forms of self-indulgence have become not only mindful but branded, strenuous, and expensive.

The term resilience was coined in the 1970s. Before that everyone was assumed to be tough, so there wasn't really a word for it.

Assertiveness training is for those afflicted by remnants of modesty.

## APOPHTHEGM

Personal density is directly proportional to temporal bandwidth.

Togetherness is largely a middle class value.

What the public wants is the image of passion, not passion itself.

Celebrity is not leadership, and is not transferable.

The only important attribute of celebrity is that it is celebrated; no one can say why.

The ordinary is what happens when we are concentrating on something else.

You have to choose your irrationality or it will choose you.

The simulation of infantile cravings by advertising, by usurpation of parental authority by the media and the school, and the rationalisation of inner life accompanied by the false promise of personal fulfilment, have created a new type of social individual.

Everything conspires to encourage escapist solutions to the psychological problems of dependence, separation, and individuation, and to discourage the moral realism that makes it possible for human beings to come to terms with existential constraints to their power and freedom.

Everyone is afraid and even the people that everyone is afraid of. This is what it really means to all be in it together.

### Violence is not simply associated with the family; it is identical to it

Without paternal authority, a child cannot develop an autonomous moral stance which would enable him to gain some kind of ethical autonomy to critically oppose society.

Parenting is a skill required by all those brave enough to endure the sacrifices to be a parent with little money, but which can only be taught, by salaried professionals who know just how, when, in what proportions and in what form, reward and punishment must be applied to the child.

The education of the masses has altered the balance of forces within the family, weakening the authority of the husband in relation to the wife and parents in relation to their children. It emancipates women and children from patriarchal authority, however, only to subject them to the new paternalism of the advertising industry, the industrial corporation, and the state.

As working-class women begin to assert their rights or at least to listen to feminist ideas, their husbands see in this turn of events another blow to their own self respect, the crowning indignity heaped on the workingman by middle-class liberalism that has already destroyed his savings, bused his children to distant schools, undermined his authority over them, and now threaten to turn even his wife against him.

Cats are a soft, indestructible automaton provided by nature to be kicked when things go wrong in the domestic circle.

## Marriage is an institution for the paralysis of the sexual instinct

Love can't flourish in a society based upon money and meaningless work: it requires complete economic as well as personal freedom.

Marriage is what happens when the state gets involved in endorsing and regulating personal relationships.

A woman is the desolation of the righteous.

Betrayal already points to love. You can't betray an acquaintance.

Love is necessary but not sufficient; love without authority does not make a conscience.

The one measure of true love is you can insult the other.

Contemporary dating culture and the online sites encourage the single to describe their tastes and preferences, indulge their narcissism, and to search for a mirror rather than for the other.

Comparing qualities of respective candidates, deciding with whom to fall in love, cannot be love.

There is no seduction which cannot at some point be construed as intrusion or harassment because there will always be a point when one has to expose oneself and make a pass. But, of course, seduction doesn't involve incorrect harassment throughout. When you make a pass, you expose yourself to the potential partner, and her reaction will determine whether what you just did was harassment or a successful act of seduction. There is no way to tell in advance what her response will be — which is why assertive women often despise weak men, who fear to take the necessary risk. This holds even more in our politically correct times: the politically correct prohibitions are rules which, in one way or another, are to be violated in the seduction process. Isn't the seducer's art to accomplish the violation in such a way that, afterwards, by its acceptance, any suggestion of harassment has disappeared?

Everything in life is about sex, except sex. Sex is about power.

The total amount of undesired sex endured by women is probably greater in marriage than in prostitution.

Consensual sex is not the same as wanted sex. And conversely, it is not the same thing as unwanted sex.

## Feminism has become the dinner-party etiquette of the liberal elite

Feminism is proliferating essentially as merchandise; we can buy anything that suits us and nothing that we really need.

The aim of liberal feminism is meritocracy, not equality. Liberal feminism is focused on *leaning in* and *cracking the glass ceiling*. However, it only enables a privileged few to climb the corporate ladder or the ranks of the military, and it subscribes to a market-centred view of equality that dovetails with corporate enthusiasm for diversity.

I have no interest in breaking the glass ceiling, while leaving the majority of women to clean up the shards.

Popularity replaced purity as the measure of a woman's social value.

*Elle* says to women: you are worth just as much as men; and to men: your women will never be anything but women.

Determinism is no friend of feminism.

If women think they are emancipated, they may want to consider the idea of tasting their own menstrual blood. If it makes them sick, they have got a long way to go.

The male to female transaction is difficult complete since the transsexual body interprets the surgically created vagina as a wound which it tries to close.

There is the basic LGBT (Lesbian, Gay, Bisexual, Transgender); LGBTQIA (Lesbian, Gay, Bisexual, Transgender, Questioning, Intersex, Asexual); and, LGBTQQIAAP (Lesbian, Gay, Bisexual, Transgender, Queer, Questioning, Intersex, Asexual, Allies, Pansexual).

My main reason for opposing gay marriage is once your friends get married, you lose them.

The angry gays don't like me, but the angry gays don't like anybody. My theory on the angry gays is they're not really gay: they just hate their fathers.

To call a man an animal is to flatter him. He is a walking dildo.

Just because you are a man who reads Julia Kristeva doesn't mean you are not sexist.

When you are subjected to endless violence, in every situation, every moment of your life, you end up reproducing it against others, in other situations, by other means. One of the instruments of this daily violence is the cult of masculinity.

## APOPHTHEGM

## State surveillance is driven by fear. Corporate surveillance is driven by money

We are legitimising a culture of universal surveillance.

Opting out of surveillance capitalism is like opting out of electricity — you are free to do it in theory. In practice, it will upend your life.

The all-powerful state install the surveillance society not to control the body, but to imprison the individual in the gaze of power.

The secret point of money and power is neither the things that money can buy nor power for power's sake, but absolute personal freedom, mobility and privacy.

The more people avoid surveillance, the more incentive corporations and governments have to devote their superior resources to developing counter-tactics, thus quickly closing off whatever vulnerabilities were revealed.

The National Security Agency vision statement is: keep the problem going so the money keeps flowing. So every time an attack happens and people get killed, they say, "We need more money."

Mechanised surveillance had become the economic basis of the modern technology industry.

Surveillance is a zero sum game. The actual value of the data collected is not clear, but it's definitely an advantage to collect more than your rivals do.

Obfuscation consists of ways the weak can temporarily elude the predations of the powerful, and it is justified with reference to that disparity. However, the tactics of obfuscation do nothing to decrease the asymmetries of power and information they are designed to disrupt. At best, they only pollute the databases of the powerful, and spur them to do a better job justifying their data collection and analysis and clarifying exactly what good they are doing. Privacy-based obfuscation negates the tendency to protest: it caters to a self-protectiveness that runs counter to the self-sacrifice that civic engagement often requires.

Obfuscation intends to spread disinformation at the expense of data collectors, it also undermines the information channels we rely on for social cohesion.

Big Data has developed its own forms of compensation to offer the populations it has conquered. For the sorts of people who are conditioned to believe (by dint of habitus, wealth, or some other type of cultural privilege) that they have nothing to hide and thus nothing to fear from being closely watched, constant surveillance can serve as a flattering form of social recognition.

By various means of seduction, coercion, and co-optation, everyday life has been irresistibly colonised by forces collectively known as Big Data: the corporations and state agencies that use communications networks and digital surveillance to amass huge quantities of information on the activities of individuals and groups in hopes of predicting and containing their next moves. Short of a total renunciation of the now routine conveniences of contemporary life and voluntary exile from the spaces where all social belonging and recognition takes place, you cannot escape.

Risk aversion has infused public and private life to such an extent that we now think of ourselves as too incompetent to act upon the world. This renders us incapable of overcoming the problems and challenges that face us. The result? We have become unfree.

No matter what laws are enacted against speech and other means of expression, citizens will continue to say what they believe, only now they will do so in secret.

## The pursuit of followers on Twitter is an occupation of the bourgeoisie

The real reason the media is rising up against Donald Trump is that he challenges their role as gatekeepers.

The exact same forces which are good for journalism and good for owners of media companies are the forces which are bad for journalists themselves, and that the chances of an individual journalist

## APOPHTHEGM

leveraging her career into a middle-class lifestyle have probably never been lower.

The newspaper is not only a collective propagandist and agitator, but also a collective organiser.

The demand to consume ideology is not the same as a desire to be informed.

Journalistic practice is placed under the exigencies of speed and constant renewal. This disposition is reinforced by the temporal nature of journalism itself, which requires living and thinking on the quick, favouring a permanent amnesia, the negative side to the celebration of the latest news and judgements based purely on new and old categories.

There can't be socialism with social media.

Facebook users are no more a reliable gauge of what is newsworthy than American Idol audiences were suited to serve as a war-crimes tribunal.

Opportunism is the bedrock principle of progressive journalism. Not the uncomplicated, self-serving kind, but the well-meaning, deluded kind that believes above all in maintaining credibility with the powerful.

Fact-checking is the foundation of a house called Enlightenment, which without it can't stand.

We do not necessarily understand messages, adverts or stories — even if they are tailored to our worldview or personalities — in the way the sender wants us to understand them.

The original selective pressure driving the spread of the language capacity in our early forebears was not its utility for communication, but rather the vastly increased conceptual ability it granted its possessors. Thus, language evolved for thought rather than communication, and its use in communication came later in our evolutionary history.

Propaganda is speech that irrationally closes off certain options that should be considered.

Balanced reporting is the ethical duty of media organisations to ensure that some chosen people will face other chosen people on a see-saw of approved alternatives.

Nothing of great importance to human values hangs on truths that everyone can accept.

Not everyone who is able to speak can speak truth.

To give up on truth was to give up on ethics.

The truth is terrible: (1) the terrible *existential* truths about the human situation (the inevitability of death and suffering); (2) the terrible *moral* truth that life is essentially something amoral; and (3) the terrible *epistemic* truth that most of what we think we know about the world around us is illusory.

The financial markets that are today our nearest thing to a regime of truth.

It makes little sense to demand transparency: the appointment of committees of inquiry, mediators, observers, high authorities of all kinds; what we need to demand is the truth.

Everything is lies. You are being fed lies every day and most of them you go along with because it's just easier, or it doesn't matter to you, or the people who are supposed to explain to you that you are being lied to are held back by, yes, paychecks, fear, ignorance, or some combination thereof. Everything's a scam. I'll be charitable: most of the people who go along with the scam aren't bad, they're just afraid of looking dumb.

## Amanda Knox

There are those who believe in my innocence.
And there are those who believe in my guilt.
There's no in between.
And if I'm guilty, it means that I am the ultimate figure to fear.

## APOPHTHEGM

Because I'm not the obvious one.
But on the other hand, if I'm innocent, it means that everyone's vulnerable.
And that's everyone's nightmare.
Either I'm a psychopath in sheep's clothing, or I am you.

## Piracy is commerce without its folly-swaddles, just as god made it

Law used to rest on an adversary relation between the state and the offender and acknowledged the superior power of the state by giving important procedural advantages to the defendant.

Imagine if there were an alternate dystopian reality where law enforcement was 100% effective, such that any potential offenders knew they would be immediately identified, apprehended, and jailed. How could people have decided that marijuana should be legal, if nobody had ever used it? How could states decide that same-sex marriage should be permitted?

The law is always prepared to lend you a spare brain in order to condemn you without remorse, and it depicts you as you should be, and not as you are.

Under ancient Jewish law, if a suspect on trial was unanimously found guilty by all judges, then the suspect was acquitted. This reasoning sounds counterintuitive, but the legislators of the time had noticed that unanimous agreement often indicates the presence of systemic error in the judicial process, even if the exact nature of the error is yet to be discovered. They intuitively reasoned that when something seems too good to be true, most likely a mistake was made. This is the paradox of unanimity.

Law cannot dispense with the use of force and is always founded in the last instance on the right of those who are strongest, which only sometimes, and contingently, coincides with the right of those who are most just.

## Silicon Valley in 2018 and the Soviet Union in 1970

Waiting years to receive a car you ordered, to find that it's of poor workmanship and quality.

Promises of colonising the solar system while you toil in drudgery day in, day out.

Five adults living in a two bedroom apartment.

Being told you are constructing utopia while the system crumbles around you.

Totally not illegal taxi taxis by private citizens moonlighting to make ends meet.

Everything is done to the needs of the military-industrial complex.

Mandatory workplace political education.

Productivity largely falsified to satisfy appearance of sponsoring elites.

Deviation from mainstream narrative carries heavy social and political consequences.

Networked computers exist but they're really bad.

Henry Kissinger visits sometimes for some reason.

Elite power struggles result in massive collateral damage, sometimes purges.

Failures are bizarrely upheld as triumphs.

Otherwise extremely intelligent people just turning the crank because it's the only way to get ahead.

The plight of the working class is discussed mainly by people who do no work.

The United States as a whole is depicted as evil by default.

The currency most people are talking about is fake and worthless.

The economy is centrally planned, using opaque algorithms not fully understood by their users.

# IV
# Electability

## The mendacity of hope

The impact of Obama's tenure can be looked at in three ways: as an agency of change at home; as a force of intervention abroad; and as a style of rule at large. Taking the first, what is the balance-sheet? Economically, a budgetary stimulus relayed by abundant quantitative easing and record-low interest rates pulled the United States out of recession, gradually reducing official unemployment and generating weak — but still better than any European or Japanese — growth. Banks were bailed out, no reliefs extended to under-water mortgages, criminal executives left unpunished, and the workforce participation ratio sank still further, while the top 1% of the population became proportionately even richer. Since there was no change at the Fed, and this course was already set in the last phase of the Bush Administration, not a great deal in this crisis-management was distinctive under Obama. By and large a defensive holding operation, it left the underlying impasse of the regime of accumulation in place since the 80s — declining productivity growth, long-term wage stagnation, deepening inequality, regional de-industrialization — essentially unaltered.

Socially, the principal legislative achievement of the Presidency was the Affordable Care Act, which extended medical coverage to about 20 million Americans, while leaving larger numbers — 28 million — still uninsured. The limits of this improvement, and the opaque complexity of its machinery, have meant that what ought to have been the Democrats' main claim to social progress won so little popular support that it was shunned by many, perhaps most, of their candidates for office in 2016. Minorities benefited most from the Act, but a third even of them reported a negative experience of it. Among working-class whites, fewer than one out of eight had a positive opinion of its impact. The parameters of the distribution of health-care changed more than those of national income. But a market-driven system unique in the West, bloated in costs and meagre in coverage, remains structurally unaltered. Under it, also unique in the West, mortality rates among working-class whites — despair deaths from drugs or suicide, typically under conditions of financial pressure — have continued to rise.

Ecologically, unable to pass a market-friendly sale of licences to pollute through Congress, Obama fell back on a patchwork of executive regulation, to little effect, and a climate change accord in Paris that, like its predecessor at Kyoto, lacks an enforcement mechanism. Unable, too — like Bush — to get immigration reform through Congress, he sought by executive fiat to suspend expulsion of one past cohort of minors, a move blocked in the judiciary, while deporting some 2.5 million other illegals from the country, more than any other President in history. Racially, was there any significant improvement in conditions of Afro-American life? Certainly not in treatment by the police: black riots in response to shootings marked Obama's tenure, not his predecessor's. Economically, towards the end of his spell in office, the net wealth of median white households was thirteen times that of black, and nearly half of black assets had vanished. Did Black Lives Matter receive anything more than grudging expressions of sympathy from the White House? Delegates were told to be thankful for the privilege of an audience: after all, he reminded them, you are sitting in the Oval Office, speaking to the President of the United States.

The contrast with Same Sex Marriage speaks for itself. There the Obama White House was flood-lit in rainbow colours, with much talk of historic progress, for a far smaller, but on average much richer, minority of the population, in a cause that (vide likewise Hollande or Cameron) is economically and socially costless, involving no loss to anyone. As for civil rights in any wider sense, Obama presided over the largest domestic (and, of course, foreign) surveillance programme in history, granted immunity to torturers while meting out savage punishment to whistle-blowers, eradicated Americans abroad without due process, and made a mockery of the War Powers Act. Constitutionally, the legislature was by-passed with a mass of ultra vires directives, even legal friends of the Administration complaining of Obama's way with presidential powers.

Admirers of Obama excuse the domestic failure of his Presidency to represent anything like an audacity of hope on the grounds of Republican obstruction in Congress. Abroad, the executive is essentially untrammelled. Predictably enough, like most of his predecessors since 1945 — Johnson and Reagan were the exceptions — Obama was more consequential as a guardian of empire overseas than as agent of change at home, though it would be difficult to guess this from the tenor of liberal and most left discussion of it in the United States. There his record falls into two major departments — operations in the Muslim world, and dealings with Russia and China (with Europe and Japan as respective helpmeets).

In the Muslim world, Obama inherited two declared wars, in Iraq and Afghanistan, and two undeclared wars, in Pakistan and Somalia. By the end of his second mandate, he had added three more. Of those he inherited, in Iraq Bush had signed an agreement with Maliki for withdrawal of all United States troops by the end of December 2011. Three years later, as the deadline neared, the Obama Administration sought to revise this for continued stationing of an American military force in the country, but was unable to secure the immunity for its soldiers from criminal prosecution in Iraq on which it insisted. So withdrawal had to go ahead, only to be reversed two years later when Obama removed Maliki, dispatching bombers, missiles and ground troops for a second war, this time against the ISIS threat to his replacement in Baghdad. In Afghanistan, Obama had trebled the size of the American army of occupation by the end of his first term, and by the end of his second, installed a Made-in-USA government like its counterpart in Baghdad, to be protected indefinitely by a force of praetorians from the Pentagon. In Pakistan, Obama escalated military strikes with a steep increase in the use of drone missiles to wipe out targets deemed hostile, with predictable civilian loss of life, while whisking CIA staff

## APOPHTHEGM

wanted for murder out of the country. In Somalia, where another customised government was set up, covert commando and drone strikes, assisted by a secret CIA base in Mogadishu, are routine, while AFRICOM has extended American military implantation across the continent, to some 49 out of 55 African countries.

Expanding this arc of operations, Obama launched an all-out aerial attack in Libya to overthrow the Gaddafi regime, plunging the country into such chaos that, five years later, not even a standard play-set of marionettes could be assembled to run the show. In Syria, he armed, trained and funded insurgents, relying on Saudi Arabia and Qatar to furnish them with heavier weapons and more money, in a bid to bring down the Assad regime, in the process fanning a civil war that has left half a million dead and five million displaced, without succeeding in dislodging his target. In Yemen, he supplied the weapons, guidance and strategic cover for a Saudi-Emirati bombing campaign that has reduced the country and its people to ruins, with a callousness that caused even his habitual barkers at the New York Times to flinch.

Nowhere has the mendacity of hope been more brazen than in these actions, Obama promising that his Libyan blitz would be just humanitarian assistance, not regime change, and that he was 'proud of his decision' not to launch a similar blitz on Syria, from which he was stayed only by the opposition of the British parliament and Congress. Elsewhere, arms and money have flowed to an Egyptian regime little different from the Syrian, simply more pro-Western; while Israel has received the largest military aid package in its history. In the imperial repertoire, a preference for air war, proxies and special forces rather than ground troops is no novelty: it was Nixon who introduced the type of *Vietnamization* under way in Kabul and elsewhere. None of Obama's seven wars have been won, in the sense of achieving a peace, though also none have been lost. One major success was registered. Concerted cyberwarfare, covert assassination and economic strangulation forced the clerical rulers of Iran to submit to an American diktat safeguarding the Israeli nuclear monopoly in the Middle East, even if this has not been followed by cooperation from Teheran in putting an end to Assad.

Inheriting the arrival of a conciliatory Russian counterpart in Medvedev, and the second term of the low-key Hu–Wen regime in China, how did Obama handle America's relations with its two former Cold War foes? After intervening in Kiev to set up a government to United States specifications, he imposed sanctions on Moscow for responding with a recovery of the Crimea, dragooning Europe behind him, and bringing Western relations with Moscow to a post-Cold War low — so far with little to show for it, other than Russian blow-back in Syria, signs of increasing unease in Europe, and a trillion dollar modernization of the American nuclear arsenal to come. In the Far East, the Administration worked to force out Yukio Hatoyama, the only Japanese premier to question the United States military grip on Okinawa, and sought to isolate the People's Republic of China by rounding up Japan, the Republic of Korea and Association of Southeast Asian Nations for a Pacific trade pact excluding China, whose commercial prospectus was always subordinate to its strategic purpose. The scheme fell apart as Obama's tenure petered out, leaving Washington–Beijing relations in neutral at the end of it. In the dying months of his rule, when there was no longer any political cost to him, diplomatic relations were restored with Havana and a UN motion condemning Israeli settlements awarded an abstention: departing gestures designed to gild his memory, along with holding hands in Hiroshima and dancing the tango in Buenos Aires. The embargo on Cuba and the United States carceral base in Guantánamo remain.

Overall, Obama's performance in office looks like most American presidencies since Reagan, not altering all that much at home while pressing ahead with imperial tasks abroad — in effect, a largely conventional stewardship of neo-liberal capitalism and military-diplomatic expansionism. No new direction for either society or empire emerged under him. Obama's rule was in this sense essentially stand-pat: business as usual. On another plane, however, his tenure was innovative. For he is the first celebrity President — that is, a politician whose very appearance was a sensation, from the earliest days of his quest for the Democratic nomination onwards: to be other than purely white, as well as good-looking and mellifluous, sufficed for that. Catapulted into the White House on colour charisma and economic crisis, and commanding the first congressional supermajority since Carter, Obama in office continued to be an accomplished vote-winner and champion money-raiser. But celebrity is not leadership, and is not transferrable. The personality it projects allows no diffusion. Of its nature, it requires a certain isolation. Obama, relishing his aura and aware of the risks of diluting it, made little attempt to mobilise the populace who cast their ballots for him, and reserved the largesse showered on him by big money for further acclamation at the polls. What mattered was his personal popularity. His party hardly counted, and his policies had little political carry-through.

The result was a debacle at each mid-term election. By the end of his rule, Obama's personal approval ratings were touching 60 per cent, while the Democratic Party had lost close to 1,000 seats in legislatures across the country, was down to 18 governorships and 12 state houses out of 50, and in public opinion the Affordable Care Act was more albatross than catnip. Celebrity dazzled, but didn't convert. To keep it intact, Obama shunned press conferences where he might be challenged, preferring instead to commune with obsequious talk-show hosts, confide to a circle of chosen sycophants in print and surround himself with star-dust from the pop charts on state occasions. In this universe, the most important official in the White House became Obama's ghost-writer, the first in American history to be promoted straight from boiler-plate to bombardier as Deputy National Security Advisor.

With the end of his Presidency in sight, homages came thick and fast across the media. Leading the field, the New York Times published a series of six extended encomia, lavish visuals of the President adorning each — *The Regulator, The Threat to the Planet, Fractured World Tested the Hope of a Young President, Finding His Voice on Race, The Health-Care Revolution, A Changed Man* — followed by full-dress sunday review treatment of *The Obama Years*, topped off with an affecting study of *How Reading Nourished Obama in Office*. Little of empirical substance was to be found in any of these. Their most significant contribution, signalled in the title of the third, was to add to the standard case that Obama had been frustrated from still greater achievements at home by obstruction in Congress, the claim that noble aims abroad had likewise been thwarted by the recalcitrance of a backward and bar-

barous world, incapable of living up to his enlightened objectives. But for the most part, in keeping with the style of the ruler himself, the emphasis of a tidal wave of threnodies fell elsewhere. Logically, their leitmotif was simply the luminous sheen of the person, rather than anything he actually did. In the words of a Nobelist in the Financial Times — "The man has a lot of class", even if "he may not have been a very effective president".

It was just such a presidency that paved the way for another celebrity to capture the White House, paying still less attention to the party that was a vehicle for getting him there. Obama's share of responsibility in Trump's path to victory was not, of course, confined to this. It was he who made Clinton's wife his Secretary of State, without any need to do so other than to gratify the couple and their wealthy establishment backers, and he who appointed the DNC which laboured to ensure she was the Democratic candidate to succeed him. The notoriously damaged and unpopular second Clinton was his choice, foisted on primary voters reluctant from the beginning to accept her, and shielded by his Department of Justice from the penal consequences visited on the humblest of leakers in his Administration, unlike her acting for public-spirited reasons, not arrogant personal privilege. Finally and decisively, of course, it was his insensibility to growing popular distress and collusion with the financial and commercial order responsible for it that created the conditions of a vehement political revolt against the establishment of which he had become so prized an ornament. Hopes that Obama would bring transformation with any ounce of audacity were always illusory. Fears that Trump will bring disaster with tons of bigotry and brutality may be more realistic, though they could prove exaggerated too. One thing, however, is clear: productive resistance to the second can have no truck with the cult of the first, which requires cold demolition.

## Political efficacy is one thing. Intellectual cogency another

Political science is a discipline which avoids politics while failing to achieve science.

Politics is war by less violent means.

# APOPHTHEGM

Being apolitical merely reinforces the status quo, supporting the powerful over the weak.

To experience politics is to experience powerlessness.

Political power is itself an illusion in the era of the neoliberal state.

Today we have more freedom and also less power.

It is key to distinguish between *politics* — the competition for and exercise of power — and *political*, which he defined as the symbols societies use to render social relations tangible.

There is no real politics that is not in and through the people itself — politics cannot claim to transcend the people, but must develop, see itself and watch itself through the people.

For the champions of political philosophy, the intellectuals seeking to shore up the established order, there is always the same difficulty to navigate: how to make people believe that their aim is to change everything, when what they want is precisely for nothing to change.

For the affluent professionals who are the Social Democracy truest believers, what is unfolding today is a scenario of fulfilment and triumph. They have always believed that politics is really just a battle between the stupid and the smart, the ignorant and the enlightened, and every morning their newspapers will tell them how very right they are.

A real material change has taken place in the capitalist mode of production that renders conventional policy tools ineffective and useless. It is not just that bourgeois parties refuse to deliver on their promises, they can't deliver on their promises. And this means a radical program for change is on an even playing field with bourgeois parties.

The cult of pragmatism justifies modern social policy unwillingness or inability to make far-reaching plans for the future.

The foreclosure of any meaningful political sphere is to the significant disadvantage of the left.

Trying to enact policies that level the playing field is the wrong approach. What's needed is to change the rules of the game, so that the measure of success is not a competitiveness that undermines solidaristic and egalitarian values.

We live in an era where everything seems possible when it comes to technology, yet nothing seems possible when it comes to politics.

Electoral victory only gives one the right to rule, not the power to rule.

Politics will always remain structurally akin to mass production, and as a consequence compare unfavourably to the ease and freedom of choice in modern consumer markets.

Two political camps have been formed in all rich countries: the camp of ideologically cosmopolitan rich whose incomes keep on increasing and the camp of nativist lower-middle classes who feel that nobody is defending their interests. This produces political polarisation with clear dangers of transforming democracy into either a plutocracy that would continue with current policies, or alternatively a populist regime that would give way to the frustration of the middle classes by re-imposing tariff rates, exchange controls and tighter migration rules.

The Third Way project was consistently bourgeois and cosmopolitan in outlook.

Trumpism is unspeakable. On the other hand the *status quo* is silence and death.

Political communities are republics that cannot by their very nature be turned into markets, or not without depriving them of some of their central qualities. Unlike the highly flexible communities of choice that emerge in societies governed by advanced patterns of consumption, political communities are basically communities of fate. At their core, they ask their members not to insist on their separate individuality but to accept a collectively shared identity, integrating the former into the latter. Compared to market relations, political relations are therefore by necessity rigid and persistent; they emphasise, and must emphasise, strong ties of duty rather than weak ties of choice. They are obligatory rather than voluntary, dialogical rather than monological, demanding sacrifices in utility and effort; and they insist on loyalty.

## Donald Trump is the best entertainment we have

Donald Trump is a liberal fantasy gone wrong.

Donald Trump is too incoherent to be a fascist.

Donald Trump is a neofascist catastrophe but Hillary Clinton would have been a neoliberal disaster.

Donald Trump's frenzied populism couldn't exist without the suffocating liberal condescension of a Hillary Clinton; nobody would ever vote for Clinton if it weren't for the looming threat of a Trump.

Donald Trump has broken the neoliberal, technocratic, political correct discourse that gave credibility to the current political class.

Donald Trump proudly endorses torture without evasive euphemisms. He promises to use waterboarding and a hell of a lot worse, not because torture works, but because even if it doesn't work, they deserve it anyway.

Jean-Marie Le Pen was capable of defending his ideas even if they weren't popular. His daughter defends what is popular whatever the ideas.

Formed in 1972, the Front National first breakthroughs came in the mid-1980s — coinciding with the abandonment by the Socialist Party of its working-class base.

Macron is presented as France's version of Trudeau or Obama, or for those with selective memories, Blair.

Tony Blair thought he could be the man who helped turn a historically enormously fractious area into a region of grateful (neo)liberal democracies, that he could impose this via bombing, and that history would look kindly upon him for it. Put as starkly as that, it seems fucking ludicrous, doesn't it? The colonial dream of an idiot. But that's what he thought. All the conspiracy theories make him look more cunning than he was.

Tony Blair was a charismatic politician who had a one-night stand with history and thought it was in love with him.

Tony Blair lost the Labour party three million votes between 1995 and 2005, Gordon Brown a further one million.

Tony Blair relied on the corrupt servility of his MPs and the supine credulity of the media to enlist their support for the Iraq War.

Brexit closes the loop on Blair's 1997 election win, and is the end of a 19-year managerial experiment.

Varoufakis prediction before the Brexit vote: in the event of Brexit, the UK will probably end up with Boris Johnson as prime minister and negotiate more rapid entry into the transatlantic trade and investment partnership.

By mid 2011, Barack Obama had attended more fund-raisers than Carter, Reagan, the first Bush and Clinton combined, and was on course to overtake all five of his immediate predecessors put together — the second Bush included — in their re-election bids.

Barack Obama was the very last horoscope candidate — a politician who managed to speak so vaguely that his platform could mean anything to anyone.

At a moment when the United States faced convulsive social crises, and more and more of his supporters called for a fundamental reconstruction of American institutions, Obama marshalled his personal story and oratorical gifts to defend hollow tenets: the righteousness of American primacy, the legitimacy of global market liberalism, the need for incremental reform, the danger of large-scale structural overhaul. The consequence was that fundamental problems continued to fester and became harder to ignore: mass incarceration and structural racism, dramatic class disparities in power and opportunity, interventionism abroad, and national-security abuses at home. Obama's domestic reforms all fell within the same philosophy that long informed the American century: faith in markets and in technocratic and national security experts (despite the repeated and catastrophic failures of all three), and suspicion of politics formed through mass democratic mobilisation. In the end, Obama's most remarkable accomplishment therefore was not the achievement of any specific policy objective — the passage of the Affordable Care Act or the killing of Osama bin Laden — but the way he infused an exhausted American centrism with new energy and attractiveness, coating a familiar brand of American liberalism with the sanctity and power of his own personal biography.

The perfect distillation of the Obama administration's approach to governance: politically rational incrementalism that reinforces the existing power structures and is grossly insufficient given the scope of the problem.

Indifferent to truth, willing to use police-state tactics and vulgar libels against inconvenient witnesses, hopeless on health care, and flippant and fast and loose with national security: the case against Hillary Clinton for president is open-and-shut. She is unable to tell the plain truth when there is any alternative.

Bernie Sanders knew he could win, but he also knew that he could not govern.

Al Gore is an old person's idea of a young person.

Richard Nixon was the only president with an original mind in foreign policy.

Richard Spencer's neo-fascist political style has not sprung directly from 1930s Germany, but as a response to Obama's cool liberal style, 4chan, new media history, alternative media's war against cultural hegemony as well as academic fetishism of anti-normativity, subculture, and transgression.

## Political parties are the mechanism through which divisions in society are argued over and competing interests asserted

The political *zeitgeist* is not defined in terms of a struggle between left and right. Party politics are meaningless in a world that rejects change and makes the state the auditor of human agency. The *zeitgeist* is a consensus, a worldview that rejects freedom in favour of security.

The party functions as a constructor, organiser and permanent persuader of the popular will.

Today's underlying rationale is that of the single party: since all accept the logic of the existing capitalist order, market economy and so forth, why maintain the fiction of opposing parties?

Conservatives punish; liberals forgive; neoliberals solve.

For the Church, a daily paper is a plus; for the party, it is a must.

The labour movement in the United States relies on the corporate-financed and corporate-led Democratic Party to promote a pro-labour political agenda.

Democratic Party is not really a party at all, but simply a framework within which candidates can run for office.

Bernie Sanders emergence as a serious challenger is an epochal development: he has shaken the Democratic Party like nothing in our lifetimes.

Trump has done nothing to change the Republican Party, but he has done everything to change the Democratic Party.

The EU referendum gave voters a unique opportunity for punishing a generation of politicians, regardless of party allegiance.

The parliamentary Labour Party, always, as a body, a pliant instrument of orthodoxy, will not become a live and powerful opposition.

The party members who voted for Corbyn hadn't suddenly thrown their toys out of the pram just because Miliband lost. This is not a story of the last five years, but the last twenty, and their disillusionment with New Labour is about a great deal more than the Iraq War. For them, Miliband was not too left-wing; on the contrary, he was a final attempt at compromise. And when it failed, they realised they had had enough. It was too difficult to go on knocking on doors, summoning the necessary conviction, working towards the slim possibility of victory in the hope of implementing a platform of ever-weakening amelioration of the worst effects of neoliberalism. They looked at the

## APOPHTHEGM

candidates on offer, and saw that they had nothing left to lose.

One of the biggest problems is, the Labour party can't think. And it never really has been able to think, of its own accord.

Of all political parties claiming socialism to be their aim, the Labour Party has always been one of the most dogmatic — not about socialism, but about the parliamentary system.

The socialist parties fit readily with capitalism, because for practical purposes they have no economic policies of their own.

Since 1981 we have had the austerity turn of 1983, privatizations, deregulation of financial markets, the Maastricht Treaty, the law on civil security, stock options: these are all fundamentals that we owe to the Socialists, so concerned still about modernisation. Hence a second difficulty: how to be credible when pretending not to be what one actually is? When Dominique Strauss-Kahn declares himself available to steer the French Socialist Party to social-democracy, or to transform the party into a modern reformist party, are they trying to make us believe that the PS is a Marxist party of revolution? How can they pretend to want to become a reformist party now, when they have always been one since the Tours congress of 1920?

Since the 1970s, both the social function and political identity of the party has been transformed in a series of stages roughly mirroring the economic dynamics of globalisation. Broadly, social democratic parties across the OECD economies have been reconstituted as elite rather than mass parties. Just as the shift of proletarian labour-power from West to East has enfeebled European and American trade unions, the disintegration of the national networks connecting labour, government and corporations has eroded the institutional basis of the classic social democratic party infrastructure. At the same time, the convergence of western elites on a common neoliberal orthodoxy has made the identities of parties less and less distinguishable in ideological terms. The result is a generalised cynicism rooted in the accurate summation that no meaningful difference exists to differentiate one group of technocratic market-managers from another. The shift to a democracy without *demos* has mirrored the neoliberal dismantling of the limited form of economic democracy — mass trade unions and collective bargaining agreements — that underpinned the *Keynesian* era.

The Greens have become a political machine of and for bobos, effectively a liberal party plus radical chic.

Far right parties improving their electoral standing is not an argument against democracy but an indictment against technocratic governance.

Journalists and academics have had a hard time understanding why the Pegida movement emerged when it did and why it has attracted so many people in Germany; there are branches of the Pegida movement in other parts of Europe, but they have gathered only marginal support thus far. Those who suggest it is driven by anger and resentment are being descriptive at best. What is remarkable, though, is that rage as a political stance has received the philosophical blessing of the leading *Alternative für Deutschland* intellectual, Marc Jongen. Jongen has not only warned about the danger of Germany's cultural self-annihilation; he has also argued that, because of the cold war and the security umbrella provided by the United States, Germans have been forgetful about the importance of the military, the police, warrior virtues — and, more generally, what the ancient Greeks called thymos (spiritedness, pride, righteous indignation, a sense of what is one's own, or rage), in contrast to eros and logos, love and reason. Germany is currently undersupplied with thymos. Only the Japanese have even less of it, presumably because they also lived through postwar pacifism. Japan can afford such a shortage, because its inhabitants are not confronted with the strong natures of immigrants. It follows that the angry Pegida demonstrators are doing a damn good thing by helping to fire up thymos in German society.

## What your government does to other countries it will eventually do to you

A government powerful enough to give its people everything is powerful enough to take it all away.

## APOPHTHEGM

When the legislative and executive powers are united in the same person, there can be no liberty.

Law does not govern. Force and the arbitrary and unchallengeable decisions of a small oligarchy, made from day to day, govern. Their decrees are the law.

The role of a president is not to make people feel safe in their emotions.

In the 80s, government was needed to fix the fact that government was the problem.

Dictating things by market research is the same as dictating by fear.

The idea that the major political and economic problems of the advanced capitalist countries derive from bad policy ideas is an absurd fairy tale.

The representative principle of the state is completely integrated into the oligarchic mechanisms that it reproduces. It certainly does not function as a means for building a popular will. Representation is all but obsolete.

The Obama administration's failure to push through a robust recovery program was a miscalculation of historic proportions and led to the 2010 congressional disaster and Donald Trump election that have defined the American political universe for the foreseeable future.

A constitution asserts that all humans possess inherent, god-given rights, and that governments exist to secure these rights.

A republican constitution isn't intended to facilitate majority rule, but rather to restrain it, whenever necessary, to secure individual liberty. A democratic constitution works the other way around.

Social standards are not legal standards and if legislature follows social prejudice, society has to become tyrannical, creating circumstances where government has the duty to make sure these practices are not legally enforced.

Bureaucracy reflects political priorities. It will never, on its own, be able to counteract power imbalances, because those imbalances will influence the laws that set the perimeters bureaucracy acts within, the priorities executives set for regulators, and the market signals that regulators look to for information.

The UK civil service is a net exporter of ideas to foreign bureaucracies. UK civil service is an expression of the management culture that has gradually taken over Whitehall since the 80s. It's a free-market conception of statecraft. It is a way of justifying the continued existence of government in an anti-government age.

Technology experts have joined economists as government's most useful idiots.

Ethics is the government of the self. Politics is the government of others.

Through the state, humans acknowledge themselves as the authors of their own destiny.

The crisis of American-style capitalism, rather than of Soviet-style state socialism, became the defining moment for projecting an alternative future. Democracy and its various institutions and values — an independent judiciary and media, checks and balances, non-discrimination, tolerance — no longer need to be retained; insofar as they could be implicated in the financial crisis, they can be identified as part of the problem rather than part of the solution. Any government taking control after 2008 should centralise political authority, limit judicial autonomy, make media outlets more beholden to the government, and bar opposition parties from controlling state institutions.

## An educated electorate is the best defence against arbitrary government

Failure to vote is the mark of the satisfied citizen.

Elected officials in our contemporary oligarchies no more represent the will of the people than did the absolutist monarchs represent the

## APOPHTHEGM

will of god.

Populism is a middle-class movement that mobilises the lower classes using radical rhetoric to attack the prevailing status quo.

The rightward shift isn't a demand coming from the electorate, it's a result of the political supply.

A notion such as electability is unthinkable without the media, which, in their every representation of a political leader, ask not only who is and is not electable, but what should be the criteria by which electability is judged.

A poll used to mean the top of your head. When voting involved assembling, counting votes required counting heads; that is, counting polls. Eventually, a poll came to mean the count itself.

Opinion polls have certain disciplinary and performative effects that reify the status quo. The polls showing radical positions as unpopular, based on the existing state of public opinion, shift the balance of power within the party so as to disadvantage those advocating for strategies to change the existing distribution of political opinion; and as the party accepts the existing distribution rather than seeking to change it, it gets reproduced.

Public-opinion polling isn't enhancing political participation. It's a form of disenfranchisement.

The growing acceptance of the therapeutic view of authority makes it possible to preserve hierarchical forms of organisation in the guise of participation.

The socio-economic status quo is widely detested. But it is regularly ratified at the polls with the re-election of parties responsible for it.

Voting in a bourgeois society only matters at the margins, but the margins matter.

Politically no other European country has so blatantly rigged an electoral system than the UK: UKIP was the largest single British party at Strasbourg under proportional representation in 2014, yet a year later, with 13% of the vote, it gained just a single seat at Westminster, while the Scottish National Party, with under 5% of the vote, took 55 seats. Under the interchangeable Labour and Conservative regimes produced by this system, voters at the bottom of the income pyramid deserted the polls. But, suddenly granted, for once, a real choice in a national referendum, they returned in force to deliver their verdict on the desolations of Tony Blair, Gordon Brown and David Cameron.

Trump and Brexit taught us something about core voters — those taken for granted by respective political parties. There is always the risk that they might decide "Why fucking bother!"

If you had told me in 2015 that a professed democratic socialist would win hundreds of thousands of votes running against Hillary Clinton, openly attack Wall Street's headlock on the Democratic Party, and actually win primaries in Michigan, Wisconsin, New Hampshire, and other states, while sweeping a host of state party caucuses, I would have guessed you were insane.

If universal suffrage by secret ballot — parliamentary democracy — is the dictatorship of the bourgeoisie, the introduction of a lottery should be deemed the dictatorship of the proletariat.

Since political participation and the expression of popular will are today no longer the predominant bases of democratic legitimacy, there is no reason to demand a planetary suffrage or representative assembly. The general accessibility of a deliberative process whose structure grounds an expectation of rational results is now more significant.

Man must, before all else, eat, drink, live and clothe himself, and then only can he engage in politics, science, art, religion, etc.; that therefore the production of the immediate material means of existence and thereby the corresponding degree of economic development of a people or a period forms the basis on which the State institutions, legal views, art and even the religious ideas of the people concerned developed and on which they therefore must be explained — and not vice-versa.

If seen in terms of customers' rights, citizenship is bound to look structurally similar to customership in the mass markets of old, as individuals must live with only some of their idiosyncratic preferences being attended to and others being compromised. Rather than just consuming political decisions, citizens in a functioning democracy are invited and indeed obliged to participate in their production. In the process, they must subject their specific, collectively unexamined raw wants to critical scrutiny in some sort of public dialogue. Getting their way may demand collective rather than individual action, requiring in turn considerable investment, making for high transaction costs without guarantee that the result will be to one's personal liking. In fact the role of citizen requires a disciplined readiness to accept decisions that one had originally opposed, or that are contrary to one's interests. Results are thus only rarely optimal from an individual's perspective, so that lack of fit with what one would have preferred must be compensated by civic satisfaction about their having been achieved through a legitimate democratic procedure. Political participation in a democracy demands, in particular, a preparedness to justify and recalibrate one's choices in the light of general principles, developing preferences not in the sense of diversifying, but rather of aggregating and unifying them. Unlike customership, citizenship demands that one provide generalised support to the community as a whole, in particular by paying taxes, which may be put to as yet undecided uses by a lawfully constituted government, as distinguished from purchases of specific goods or services paid for one at a time, at market prices.

# V
# Cogency

### Are we living in a computer simulation?

1. humans will go extinct before they have the technical capacity to create a hyper-realistic simulation.

2. an advanced civilization with the technical capacity to create a hyper-realistic historical simulation would be uninterested in doing so.

3. we are almost certainly living in a computer simulation.

### The task of philosophy is to corrupt the youth

Philosophy leaves everything as it is. It sounds like a complaint, but actually it is a recommendation.

Concepts are tools of analysis, not recognition.

The absence of philosophical foundations entails cognitive nihilism.

It is not consciousness that determines life, but life that determines consciousness.

The classical distinction between explanation and clarification, between causal or causal-sounding hypotheses and interpretation. Natural phenomena require causal explanation, of the kind given by physics, say, whereas social phenomena require elucidation — richer, more expressive descriptions. One major task of philosophy is help us

## APOPHTHEGM

get clear on this distinction and to provide the right response at the right time. This requires judgment, which is no easy thing to teach.

In the midst of so much philosophy, humanity, and civilization, and of such sublime codes of morality, we have nothing to show for ourselves but a frivolous and deceitful appearance, honour without virtue, reason without wisdom, and pleasure without happiness.

Enlightenment was the beginning of a fascinating historical experience, an era that allowed for a search for values and the emergence of original ideas, that generated new forms of government, social utopias and myriad political reforms. It was the laboratory of modernity.

European Enlightenment was a legitimate child of the *Ancien Régime* and a radical cultural revolution that was destined to become the founding event of modern Western identity leading to the steady rise of a new civilisation.

Enlightenment was humanity daring to use its critical faculties, to think for itself, without the support of tradition and authority.

The whole point of the Enlightenment is to look at the world as it is, not as we wish it to be, in order to assess our possibilities within it.

Modernism is still all about language, whereas postmodernism displaces the sensory focus from the verbal to the visual.

If modernity was the attempt to replace god, postmodernity began when we gave up on replacing god, when we accepted that there was neither a god nor a viable surrogate.

Interrogation represents the modernist position: god is dead, but that does not mean that truth, even under a totalitarian regime, is a mere subjective illusion. The postmodern world begins when we move from epistemological uncertainty to ontological uncertainty. This is when we give up on believing that there is such a thing as a stable reality beneath or amidst the created narratives. Post-truth represents the postmodernist position: you have your facts — we have alternative facts. Everything is PR.

Let's be clear: cultural Marxism is a block which comprises the Frankfurt School, the French poststructuralist deconstructionism, identity politics, gender and queer theories.

The deconstructive approach, which in different versions was predominant in the last couple of centuries, is gradually disappearing.

Western philosophy is essentially a philosophy of the state that justifies its power and thereby squashes plebian protest at its inception by making it inconceivable. Intellectuals, science, and reason are all complicit in the project of state domination. Against it, revolution is not an option because it only reinforces state power. The only defensible politics is the unreflective, self-interested action of plebian resistance.

French thought had always contained a significant strand of scientism.

China has no philosophy, only thought.

## Machiavelli was the first Western political philosopher to exclude anything divine or magical from his thinking

The cosmopolitan refugee Theodor Adorno could not have been more different from the pontificating village Nazi Martin Heidegger. Though they loathed each other profoundly, and disagreed about everything else, both agreed that fascism was the result of the Enlightenment.

The legacy of Adorno and Horkheimer has been put through the blender of Habermas's philosophy of communication.

Foucault said that Derrida practiced the method of terrorism of obscurantism. Derrida writes so obscurely you can't tell what he's saying, that's the obscurantism part, and then when you criticise him, he can always say, "You didn't understand me; you're an idiot." That's the terrorism part.

Jacques Derrida's *Of Grammatology* announced the end of the book, but it is hard not to think of it as quite a book, but as Derrida's magnum opus. The *Of Grammatology* English translation of 1976 with its manifesto-like quality, and its 100-page preface by a then relatively unknown Gayatri Chakravorty Spivak, became the book to have read across the humanities. It launched 'deconstruction' in the United States. Derrida makes a startling claim in the *Of Grammatology* : to focus on the apparently marginal and secondary issue of writing raises problems serious enough to overrun all the conceptual resources of the then triumphant human sciences (and their model of scientificity provided by structural linguistics), in addition to those of history in general and indeed philosophy itself. All these disciplines share presuppositions that a hard look at the question of writing radically unsettles. Like other seismic events of thought, Derrida's insight is quite simple, yet in its very simplicity hard to grasp. Identities in general arise out of difference, but difference is not itself any identity or indeed any thing at all. It is not that there are first things, and then differences and relations between them: the things emerge only from the differences and relations, which have an absolute priority, and that emergence is never complete. It is that insight that led to the neologism *différance*. In the beginning is *différance*, which means that there is no simple beginning or origin. And the *différance* never ends, which means that there is no simple end. Derrida's simple claim, then, is that nowhere ever is there anything simple.

Marx wrote the *Manifesto of the Communist Party* less as a Marxian economist than as a communist Ricardian.

## Argument is consistently bourgeois

Everyone identifies intellectual excellence with elitism.

Intellectual merit can be confused with the mere acquisition of professional credentials or, worse with loyalty to an unspoken ideological consensus.

Busyness makes us bad thinkers.

The pleasure of thinking is not to be recommended.

To think thoughts because it is fun seems more dignified.

Theory is theory in the authentic sense only where it serves practice. Theory that wishes to be sufficient unto itself is bad theory.

What is so seductive about postmodern theory is precisely its insistence upon subverting not just old certainties, but the very possibility of certainty itself.

An empirical approach that is unwilling to read is worth very little. It amounts to not much more than the reflexes of prejudice.

The marketplace of ideas that has been emptied of all but the approved ideological vendors.

Practical wisdom (*phrónesis*) is not simply as a technical skill, but as a capacity to undertake actions oriented towards ends, and, crucially, an ability to reflect on the consonance of means and ends with the good life. Though the practices essential to the exercise of *phrónesis* — arts, sciences, games, politics — are conducive to virtue, there is still a superiority of theoretical wisdom (*sophia*). The contemplative life of *sophia* is the truly excellent life. It is possible that this valuation of *sophia* is the source of modernity's perverse metaphysical subjectivism and that *phrónesis* is the higher calling.

The corollary of Information Overload is the Paradigm Underload. The problem facing society is not the quantity of information but the conceptual tools and paradigms with which to filter, prioritise, structure and make sense of information. Unfortunately, without a paradigm, the meaning of human experience becomes elusive to the point that the worship of Big Data displaces the quest for Big Ideas.

## Paranoia is 20th century replacement for religion

The Bible is a theological-political treatise.

Immaculate conception has nothing to do with the birth of Jesus: it is the doctrine that Mary herself was conceived by her mother (St Anne) without the stain of original sin. The virgin birth is the doctrine of Christ's birth without a human father. This is one of our most frequent errors.

## APOPHTHEGM

Jihad used by Muslims to describe three different kinds of struggle: an individual's internal struggle to live out the Muslim faith as well as possible; the struggle to build a good Muslim society; and the struggle to defend Islam, with force if necessary (holy war).

We need to take religion seriously, especially when it starts to disappear.

Religion is a pleasant fantasy for people to try and mollify the pain of the reality of existence.

People do not believe because they see, they see because they already believe.

God smiles at those he sees denouncing evils of which they are the cause.

Structures need a centre, a grounding point, be it god or some substitute, a way to limit the otherwise endless play of signifiers and the things they signify. There has to be a transcendental signified for the difference between signifier and signified to be somewhere absolute and irreducible. But this transcendental signified centre is precisely what is missing, what does not and cannot exist. The implication is both destabilising and liberating. The absence of the transcendental signified extends the domain and play of signification infinitely.

## Profanity is socially useful because it is socially risky

Everything is permitted but nothing is possible.

The more eager one is to break the taboo, the more harmless it is.

To scandalise is a right; to be scandalised is a pleasure.

Death must enter life only to define it.

In psycho-analysis nothing is true except the exaggerations.

We should live our lives in such a way that things will get better in a hundred years.

If you want to be good and do good, empathy is a poor guide.

If you focus on mortality the house always wins.

Morality is inscribed in power relations and only the modification of these power relations can bring about the modification of morality.

Company values sounds like a crisis of business confidence: companies apparently ashamed of existing to make money — and of paying labour to make it for them — hallucinate a higher calling. Invoking values instead of value, they recast themselves as something more like a religious cult, a political movement or the synthesis of the two, a Charity.

We can't avoid making moral judgements. We can't live our lives otherwise. To be a relativist is to indulge in abstention.

When we make moral judgement we are not just saying that this is better than that. We are saying that this is more important than that.

Statements of fact ("your mother gave birth to you") can never lead to moral conclusions ("so you should be nice to your mother").

Making happiness the goal of life is very vacuous. If what we want to do is maximise the state of feeling happy then all we have to do is invent a psychic aspirin that makes us happy the whole time. But, we wouldn't want to say that someone has been made perpetually happy by being drugged and that person is somehow leading a good life. We were made for something else; not to be idiotically happy the whole time. Happiness is a by-product of an achievement of doing something well, of realising your potential, flourishing, and things of that kind.

## Death destroys a man; the idea of death saves him

Alone we suffer, alone we die, and alone we must make meaning out of our fate.

The response of the tech world to death has been enthusiastic. They are going to fix it.

# APOPHTHEGM

It is precisely because life is meaningless, because it has no value or purpose imposed on it from above or outside, that the individual human being must endow it with meaning by deciding on an authentic existence.

Consciousness is a much smaller part of our mental life than we are conscious of, because we cannot be conscious of what we are not conscious of. It is like asking a flashlight in a dark room to search around for something that does not have any light shining upon it. The flashlight, since there is light in whatever direction it turns, would have to conclude that there is light everywhere. And so consciousness can seem to pervade all mentality when actually it does not.

I would retain the status of courage as a virtue — that is, not an innate disposition, but something that constructs itself, and which one constructs, in practice. Courage is the virtue which manifests itself through endurance in the impossible. This is not simply a matter of a momentary encounter with the impossible: that would be heroism, not courage. Heroism has always been represented not as a virtue but as a posture: as the moment when one turns to meet the impossible face to face. The virtue of courage constructs itself through endurance within the impossible; time is its raw material. What takes courage is to operate in terms of a different durée to that imposed by the law of the world.

## Global warming

There is a new scientific theory that warns of an impending crisis, and points to a way out. This theory quickly draws support from leading scientists, politicians, and celebrities around the world. Research is funded by distinguished philanthropies and carried out at prestigious universities. The crisis is reported frequently in the media. The science is taught in secondary schools and universities.

Its supporters include Prime Ministers and Presidents from a range of countries around the world. Research Institutes have been built to carry out research in the area, but important work is also done at Cambridge, Oxford, Sorbonne, Harvard, Yale, Princeton, Stanford, and

Johns Hopkins. Legislation to address the crisis has passed in states from New York to California.

These efforts have the support of the National Academy of Sciences, the American Medical Association, and the National Research Council. It is said that if Jesus were alive, he would have supported this effort.

All in all, the research, legislation, and moulding of public opinion surrounding the theory has been going on for half a century. Those who opposed the theory are shouted down and called anti-scientific, reactionary, blind to reality, or just plain ignorant. But in hindsight, what is surprising is that so few people objected.

Today, we know that this famous theory that gained so much support was actually pseudoscience. The crisis it claimed was non-existent. And the actions taken in the name of this theory were morally and criminally wrong. Ultimately, they led to the deaths of millions of people.

The theory was eugenics, and its history is so dreadful — and, to those who were caught up in it, so embarrassing — that it is now rarely discussed. But it is a story that should be well known to every citizen, so that its horrors are not repeated.

# VI
# Hegemony

## Stalinism

1. The role of Stalinism at home and abroad had to be distinguished. Within the USSR, the Stalinist bureaucracy played a contradictory role — defending itself simultaneously against the Soviet working-class, from which it had usurped power, and against the world bourgeoisie, which sought to wipe out all the gains of the October Revolution and restore capitalism in Russia. In this sense, it continued to act as a centrist force. Outside the USSR, by contrast, the Stalinized Comintern had ceased to play any anti-capitalist role, as its debacle in Germany had now irrevocably proved. Hence the Stalinist apparatus could completely squander its meaning as an international revolutionary force, and yet preserve part of its progressive meaning as the gate-keeper of the social conquests of the proletarian revolution. The Comintern performed an actively counter-revolutionary role in world politics, colluding with capital and shackling labour in the interests of protecting the Stalinist monopoly of power in Russia itself, which would be threatened by the example of any victory of a socialist revolution, creating a proletarian democracy, elsewhere.

2. Within the USSR Stalinism represented the rule of a bureaucratic stratum, emergent from and parasitic upon the working class, not a new class. This stratum occupied no independent structural role in the process of production proper, but derived its economic privileges from its confiscation of political power from the direct producers, within the

framework of nationalised property relations.

3. The administration over which it presided remained typologically a workers' state, precisely because these property relations — embodying the expropriation of the expropriators achieved in 1917 — persisted. The identity and legitimacy of the bureaucracy as a political caste depended on its defense of them. This, dismisses the two alternative accounts of Stalinism most widespread in the labour movement in the 1930s — that it represented a form of state capitalism or of bureaucratic collectivism. The iron dictatorship exercised by the Stalinist police and administrative apparatus over the Soviet proletariat was not incompatible with the preservation of the proletarian nature of the state itself — any more than the absolutist dictatorships over the nobility had been incompatible with the preservation of the nature of the feudal state, or the fascist dictatorships exercised over the bourgeois class were with the preservation of the nature of the capitalist state. The USSR was indeed a degenerated workers' state, but a pure dictatorship of the proletariat — conformable to an ideal definition of it — had never existed in the Soviet Union in the first instance.

4. Marxists should adopt a two-fold stance towards the Soviet state. On the one hand, there is no chance of the Stalinist regime either reforming itself or being reformed peacefully within the USSR. Its rule could only be ended by a revolutionary overthrow from below, destroying its whole machinery of privilege and repression, while leaving intact the social property relations over which it presided — if now within the context of a proletarian democracy. On the other hand, the Soviet state had to be defended externally against the constant menace of aggression or attack by the world bourgeoisie. Against this enemy, the USSR — incarnating as it did the anti-capitalist gains of October — needed the resolute and unconditional solidarity of revolutionary socialists everywhere. Every political tendency that waves its hand hopelessly at the Soviet Union, under the pretext of its non-proletarian character, runs the risk of becoming the passive instrument of imperialism.

## Marxist theory is all-powerful because it is true

The purpose of Marxism is not egalitarianism, but freedom.

The goal of the Marxist project is to put history in the hands of the people and to give them freedom from the stochasticity of history.

Marxism is an intervention in the history of freedom.

The goal of Marxism is not a society aimed at endless quantitative expansion (exchange value) but at the fulfillment of qualitative needs (use value).

From the Marxist point of view, which expresses the historical interests of the proletariat, the end is justified if it leads to increasing the power of man over nature and to the abolition of the power of man over man.

Marx refers to crises as the means by which capitalism overcomes the falling rate of profit. Which means, contrary to most Marxist perspectives, the last thing we should want are crises, no matter how necessary they appear for the formation of political consciousness.

Marxism is basically not possible unless there is the prospect of an immediate revolution.

Communist politics are nothing more than an expression in political relationship the material changes in the mode of production.

Communism is free time and nothing else.

Every Communist must grasp the truth that political power grows out of the barrel of a gun.

With the French Revolution, the communist hypothesis inaugurates the epoch of political modernity.

The goal of socialism is to overthrow capitalism, not to give answers to every little everyday issue that arises under capitalism. If the Bolsheviks sat in the Duma all day talking about legalising weed and buttfucking, the October revolution would have never happened.

# APOPHTHEGM

The Bolsheviks showed that under a strong state even a deeply backward, sprawling, agrarian economy could march towards the electric lights and blast furnaces of modernity.

Lenin's last struggle against Stalin has all the hallmarks of a proper tragedy: it was not a melodrama in which the good guy fights the bad guy, but a tragedy in which the hero becomes aware that he is fighting his own progeny, and that it is already too late to stop the fateful unfolding of his wrong decisions in the past.

In the Leninist dictatorship, one could be shot for what one said, in Stalinism one could be shot for what one did not say.

Stalin's purges were the biggest wave of anti-Communist persecution in history.

The communist regime in the USSR was often cruel, but it was still run by people, and so it was at least possible to appeal to their compassion and not impersonal like the market.

In the former USSR everything the party said about socialism was a lie, but everything it said about capitalism turned out to be true.

You know what's wrong with Spain? Modern plumbing! In healthier spiritually times, plague and pestilence could be counted on to thin down the Spanish masses. Now with modern sewage disposal and the like they multiply too fast. The masses are no better than animals, and you can't expect them not to become infected with the virus of Bolshevism.

Police officers escorting a Menshevik and a Bolshevik to prison could go off for a drink, leaving both scofflaws unsupervised because a Menshevik and a Bolshevik would invariably spend the whole time arguing with each other instead of making a dash for freedom.

## Revolution is the festival of the oppressed

There is no hegemony without the construction of a popular identity on the basis of the plurality of democratic demands.

A revolution poses an age-old plaint for our casually dispossessed masses: Who can we shoot?

For the oppressed, violence is always legitimate — since their very status is the result of violence.

A rebellion against a tyrant is only immoral when it hasn't got a chance.

He who makes a revolution by half digs his own grave.

The ultimate problems in our society require radical decision, not reasonable deliberation.

Cuteness is a way of aestheticising powerlessness.

Behind every fascism there is a failed revolution.

True revolution will not be achieved by students, because they are children of bourgeois. Revolution can only be done by workers.

Revolution is one of the half-dozen topics in this world worth writing about and the least miserable, even in the face of defeat.

Revolutionaries have to wait patiently for the very brief period of time when the system openly malfunctions or collapses, seize the window of opportunity, grab the power which at that moment as it were lies on the street, is up for grabs, and then fortify its hold on power, building repressive apparatuses, etc., so that, once the moment of confusion is over and the majority gets sober and is disappointed by the new regime, it will be too late to get rid of it, given its firm entrenchment.

It is a modernist prejudice that capitalism, as a historical epoch, will end only when a new, better society is in sight, and a revolutionary subject is ready to implement it.

The revolutionary process is not a gradual progress but a repetitive movement, a movement of repeating the beginning, again and again.

The claim that revolutionary praxis leads to totalitarian catastrophe enjoys the nearly universal assent of intellectual opinion.

## APOPHTHEGM

"At least we have done something" is the rallying cry of those who privilege self-esteem rather than effective action. The only criterion of a good tactic is whether it enables significant success or not.

The centrality of the revolution in the French imaginary enables minorities, however small, to stand for France against the majority.

Robespierre was not on the face of it nor destined to become one of the chief architects of a political experiment whose meaning has been debated ever since.

Robespierre, Danton, Marat, Fabre d'Eglantine, Saint-Just came out of nowhere: middle-class provincials with little or nothing in their backgrounds to suggest they were qualified for major parts in a great world-historical drama.

There is a problem with the English word *virtue*. It sounds pallid and Catholic. But *vertu* is not smugness or piety. It is strength, integrity and purity of intent. It assumes the benevolence of human nature towards itself. It is an active force that puts the public good before private interest.

The workers' revolt of 1848, bloodily crushed by the colonial army led by Louis Eugène Cavaignac, it was the first great massacre of workers in the streets of Paris. It was this massacre that marked a long and permanent rupture between the working class world and the figure of republicanism. It was here that the workers understood that it was not true that the republican proposition was in itself favourable to them.

The ardent revolutionaries of May 1968 imagined, like Columbus, that they were setting out for China, only to land in America — more specifically California, launching a cultural revolution in the name of a dreamland communism that in fact ushered in, rather than overthrew, a capitalism of demoralised consumption.

Every radical change ever undertaken by the radical Left since 1848 has depended on seizing political power. This could be through force of arms, elections, or mass strikes; but the strategy is always the same. First we get the power; then, something … finally, Communism!

The revolutionary surge of the 1970s ended with the terrorist spectacles staged by the likes of Baader-Meinhof and the Red Brigades — a new epoch that could dispense with ideology since capitalist hegemony now lay in a set of lifestyles, conducts, needs, demands, whose origin and end was in the world of commodities. Now there is no ethos, no directive idea, no concern with the inner life of the individual, which is delivered over to the market and the unconscious, and no need either for intellectuals and their passionate devotion to ideas. The new era's basic value is tolerance, that is, indifference.

Taliban means students. The singular is Talib.

The rich rob the poor; it's business. When the poor fight back, it's considered violence.

Some think the lack of a revolutionary movement today comes from the fact that the consciousness of workers has been obfuscated by the seductions of consumerist society and manipulation by the ideological forces of cultural hegemony. Hence, some have proposed the shift in the focus to cultural criticism (or the *cultural turn*).

Today there's no need for any mass repression since there no mass opposition to crush.

## The Left only wants the power to put its own brand of social-fascism into place

Socialism is a crude form of communism, the communism of poverty and labour. The whole of society becomes a work house and labour is merely generalised, not abolished. It is an advance relative to capital in that no one is forced to labour for another and no one can live by the labour of others.

The left has always been inclined to make predictions of its preferences.

Somehow, the Left believes it can get rid of inequality, poverty, racism and a host of social ills connected with wage slavery, yet continue to sell its labour power to capital much as before. Even the best minds on

# APOPHTHEGM

the Left assume the sale of labour power is an innocent commercial transaction that has no connection to its results.

The abolition of wage labour and production for profit should begin immediately with the assumption of power of a socialist government on its first day in office.

Socialism is the tendency inherent in an industrial civilization to transcend the self-regulating market by consciously subordinating it to a democratic society.

The purpose of the socialist project is to increase the weight of the social in determining resource allocation, as opposed to capitalism which aims at increasing the weight of the capital in determining resource allocation.

The planned economy of state socialism pay a terrible price for the privilege it accorded to production over consumption. Hence, it failed to provide consumers with goods they needed, instead of products nobody wanted.

One of the main tasks of a socialist movement is to help people overcome the narrow and oppressive identities the current system imposes on them.

The earliest socialists had little interest in the daily struggles of working people. For them, socialism was to be discovered through careful thinking, and realised by a wealthy benefactor. They waited everyday for some philanthropist to come invest in their socialist future. Charles Fourier even went so far as to pitch to Napoleon his grand scheme to rescue the human race from social chaos.

Left-liberals: the worse the situation gets, the more they feel morally superior.

The Left wants to talk about everything else in the world except the urgent necessity for the abolition of wage labour. And this is because, fundamentally, the Left accepts the bourgeois narrative that the abolition of wage labour would mean the end of human civilization.

We know capital reduces the labour time required for production of commodities, but we also know it does this only to lengthen labour time. It seems most socialists have a beef with capital that it does not do enough of the latter; their complaint seems to be that not enough labour is being artificially created by the existing state and they promise to redouble this effort.

The left moralises from a position of weakness, because it is not tough-minded enough to see power for what it really is.

If the recent past demonstrates anything to us, it is that the Left aligning with the centre is utterly useless at preventing the rise of fascism, because it means allowing the centre to perpetuate precisely the policies which give ground to fascism, while confirming the irrelevance of the Left as an oppositional pole.

If Syriza is radically left, then Olof Palme and Bruno Kreisky were Stalinists and Stalin no longer conceptually graspable since the attribute Stalinist is already applied to social democracy.

Social democracy has no alternative viable strategy, especially for big capital (and big capital has no viable alternative strategy for itself) which does not involve massive state support.

Once social democracy enters government, it is committed to finding solutions to the crisis which are capable of winning support from key sections of capital, since its solutions are framed within those limits. This requires it to use its indissoluble link with the leaderships of the trade unions, not to advance, but to discipline the class and organisations it represents.

The social democrat approach, which accepts the premises of capitalism and wage labour, has in practice led directly to neoliberalism.

Keynesianism thinks that capitalism can be made to operate at close to full employment, and thereby be made into a humane system through state intervention in demand management.

The state meets social pressure with reform, but can never go the full way; as reform reveals itself incapable of subduing pressure and protest, so does the emphasis shift towards repression, coercion, police power, law and order. But repression also engenders opposition, and along that road that lies the transition from bourgeois democracy to conservative authoritarianism.

Social democracy is dead: that great agent of consensus, the main rampart against civil war; dead across the whole world, or nearly so. In Germany, the country where it was born, it was dismantled by the Schroeder system.

The social democratic moment is over. It relied on capitalist economies that delivered mass employment and a rising standard of living for the majority of the population.

European socialists and communists had expected the accumulation of capital both to expand the size of the industrial workforce and, at the same time, to unify the workers as a social subject: the collective worker, the class in-and-for itself. However, instead of incubating the collective worker, capitalist accumulation gave birth to the separated society. The forces of atomisation overpowered those of collectivisation. Late capitalist civilisation is now destabilising, but without, as yet, calling forth the new social forces that might be able, finally, to dissolve it.

We live in the 1960s liberalism religion captured by capital.

Darwinian natural selection provided the explanation for why *laissez-faire* liberalism required a continual struggle for existence.

The liberalism lead by the professional managerial class has not only failed at destroying fascism and white supremacy, but through its cultivation of culturalist pieties and neglect of economic policies, add to the appeal of its most virulent adversaries.

The real motives of liberals have nothing to do with the welfare of other people. Instead, they have two related goals. First, to establish themselves as morally and intellectually superior to the rather distasteful population of common people; and second, to gather as much power as possible to tell those distasteful common people how they must live their lives.

Liberalism has never been interested in true, universal liberation but was instead an ideology by which privileged elites justified and celebrated their domination over workers, slaves, and conquered native peoples.

The reigning ideology of the advanced capitalist states benefits from the shift from the nation state to liberal democracy as the dominant means of discursive integration of the labouring classes.

Contemporary progressivism has come to mean papering over material inequality with representational diversity.

## The rich are more likely to be critical of democracy than the poor

From Ancient Greece, we have a name for the intrusion of the excluded into the socio-political space: democracy.

Our predicament is to live in a society that was devised as a solution to a problem we have forgotten. The democratic state once battled the church in a war over human life's basic orientation; democracy won.

The idea of democracy is built on the fundamental belief in the intelligence of the democratic individual, the belief that every individual is capable of winning the struggle against his self-incurred immaturity. Without that belief in the democratic individual, the way is clear for the tyranny of the regulative state.

The general incompatibility between capitalism and democracy is too obvious to need repetition: capitalism is a spontaneous system driven by its own immanent tendencies, while the essence of democracy lies in people intervening through collective political praxis to shape their destinies, including especially their economic destinies, which militates against this spontaneity.

Democracy has been increasingly portrayed as a horrible mistake, the unworkable aspiration of starry-eyed dreamers that is pre-programmed to end in chaos.

## APOPHTHEGM

Democracy has become the unsurpassable horizon of our time.

Democratic republic is the ideal political shell for capitalism.

The ultimate enemy today is not capitalism, empire or exploitation, but democracy. It is the acceptance of democratic mechanisms as the ultimate frame that prevents a radical transformation of capitalist relations.

Where democracy is reckoned any threat to capital, the United States and its allies have never hesitated to remove it.

The supposed triumph of democracy after the implosion of the barracks of communism was accompanied by a gradual dissolution of the sense of this word, which has come to denote indifferently both the collapse of thinking and the programmed consumption of cultural goods and organic products: the democratisation of philosophy via philosophy cafés and *Philosophie* magazine, the democratisation of smoked salmon via promotions at Carrefour.

Democracy is fundamentally a political formula.

## Xenophobia is the socialism of fools

The poor are not more racist than the middle class, they are just more obviously so.

The moral face-off between good and evil is a recent invention that evolved in concert with modern nationalism and it gives voice to a political vision not an ethical one.

Every age has its fascism.

Populism is on the rise across the globe not because citizens feel empowered by new technologies, but because they feel disempowered by everything else.

In the 1920s, the revolutionary subjects, the masses and the Party, disintegrated and both went in bad directions. The masses to Fascism and the Party to Stalinism.

The old world is dying, and the new world struggles to be born: now is the time of monsters.

The European Common Market is not a reaction against and away from fascism and the epoch of imperialist savagery by the bourgeoisie; it is more like a sort of etherealised fascism, minus the uniforms, the anti-semitism, the Führer, the party dictatorship, and other old folklore.

Racism is now reflexive. Consider the Balkans. They are portrayed in the liberal Western media as a vortex of ethnic passion — a multiculturalist dream turned into a nightmare. The standard reaction of a Slovene is to say: "yes, this is how it is in the Balkans, but Slovenia is not part of the Balkans; it is part of *Mitteleuropa*; the Balkans begin in Croatia or in Bosnia; the Slovenes are the last bulwark of European civilisation against the Balkan madness." If you ask, "Where do the Balkans begin?" you will always be told that it begins down there, towards the south-east. For Serbs, they begin in Kosovo or in Bosnia where Serbia is trying to defend civilised Christian Europe against the encroachments of this Other. For the Croats, the Balkans begin in Orthodox, despotic and Byzantine Serbia, against which Croatia safeguards Western democratic values. For many Italians and Austrians, they begin in Slovenia, the Western outpost of the Slavic hordes. For many Germans, Austria is tainted with Balkan corruption and inefficiency; for many Northern Germans, Catholic Bavaria is not free of Balkan contamination. Many arrogant Frenchmen associate Germany with Eastern Balkan brutality — it lacks French finesse. Finally, to some British opponents of the European Union, Continental Europe is a new version of the Turkish Empire with Brussels as the new Istanbul — a voracious despotism threatening British freedom and sovereignty.

Canada sells itself as one of the most multicultural countries in the world. It is true that many religions, skin tones, and languages coexist there. But, as in most places, the diversity stops there. The immigration system has already filtered the worthy candidates that can adapt to the friendly and generous Canadians. That cab driver used to be a doctor in Islamabad. That engineer's parents were the upper one percent

# APOPHTHEGM

in China. There is no diversity in any of this. No varied modes of life. Either a skilled worker, a technocrat, or a capitalist. Economies cannot tolerate cultures that are counter to production. Sub-cultural modes can co-exist, home languages can remain intact, but material culture still has to fit in the dominant modes of production, consumption, and exchange. Cultural forms that cannot be commodified are simply not sustainable.

Unlimited tolerance must lead to the disappearance of tolerance.

One of the great ironies of the civil rights and feminist movements was that, just as banks and credit-card companies were pressed to develop colour- and gender-blind risk models — creating greater equality of opportunity for getting into debt — they also subjected more and more people to the patterns of discipline and crisis within contemporary financial markets.

Wage labour is no less an abomination than segregation was in the 1950s.

Far from representing the ultimate rejection of democratic ideals, fascist movements have consistently presented themselves as the democratic alternative to liberalism.

Adolf Eichmann had a good lot of good sense. What was he lacking then? He did not say no right away, at the beginning, when he was a mere administrator, a bureaucrat. He might have said to some of his friends "I don't really like Himmler." He might have whispered something, the way it's done in publishing firms, newspaper offices, in sub-government, in the newsrooms. Or he might even have objected to the fact that some train had stopped once a day for the deported to do their business, for bread and water, when two stops might have been more practical and economic. But he never stopped the machine.

When the Nazis attacked the communists, I was a little uneasy, but, after all, I am not a communist, so I did nothing. Then they attacked the socialists, I was a little uneasier, but, still, I was not a socialist, and I did nothing. Then the schools, the press, the Jews, and soon, and I was always uneasy, but still I did nothing. And then they attacked the church, and I was a churchman, and I did something, but then it was too late.

# VII
# Value

## Theory of money

1. Value or the socially necessary labour time required for production of a commodity cannot be seen or measured directly; it can only appear in the form of exchange value.

2. Exchange value itself is the measure of the value one commodity expressed in the physical form of another commodity.

3. Over time a single commodity emerges that becomes the universally valid expression of the values of all other commodities — a money commodity.

4. In circulation of commodities this money commodity is represented by a token, a valueless symbol of money that stands in for it; this token, having no value of its own, is not itself exchange value, but only the symbolic representative of exchange value, of money, in circulation.

5. The actual value represented by this token is determined by the quantity of a commodity money for which it can be redeemed; thus commodity money serves as the standard for all prices denominated in a fiat currency.

6. The forcible increase by the state of the quantity of currency in circulation does not have any impact on the quantity of value in circulation, but, instead, reduces the value symbolically represented by each unit of the currency.

Thus, the purchasing power of the currency could be diluted (depreciated), just as easily as a fool can dilute a fine scotch by adding ice.

## The *laissez faire* economy is the product of deliberate state action

The declaration of the end of the Bretton Woods system highlighted that the principles of free trade, the fee market and solidarity of the free world could not stand in the way of the national interest.

Capitalism or Marxism came to an end when Nixon announced the closing of the gold window in August 15, 1971. After all, *Das Kapital* clearly says that money — in the form of precious metal — remains the foundation from which the credit system, by its very nature, can never detach itself.

The fundamental insight of political economy is forgotten: that the natural laws of the economy, which appear to exist by virtue of their own efficiency, are in reality nothing but projections of social power relations which present themselves ideologically as technical necessities.

In economics, there are two solutions. Either you are a Leninist. Or you won't change anything.

State control of production renders the entire capitalist class superfluous. And no one wants to be superfluous.

How much more centralised can production be without the state actually telling each factory what to produce? The only reason why the state doesn't do this last is that it is the national capitalist and as such is not the least bit concerned with production of use values. The state as capitalist is only concerned with the production of surplus values, not use values. It is no surprise that the state doesn't micro-manage each factory's production, because it is concerned about the production of surplus value as a whole. It treats the whole of the national labour force as a single undifferentiated labour power, from which it extracts surplus value.

The issue of the 21ˢᵗ century is not centralisation versus decentralisation of the economy, because the entire economy has already been centralised under the control of the state and managed through its economic policies. The state literally sets prices and interest rates through its economic policy tools, determines critical production decisions and controls national trade through trade deals.

Economists have a tendency to answer criticism with accusations of a lack of understanding.

Don Quixote long ago paid the penalty for wrongly imagining that knight errantry was compatible with all economical forms of society.

Recklessness is only dangerous if it is bad for business.

Crises are not a necessary feature of the capitalist mode of production, but only a means to temporarily re-establish conditions for the normal operation of the mode of production.

Capitalist crisis erupt, because the profit rate falls and investment halts, however the fall in the rate of profit is not produced by either under-consumption or over-production, but because less living labour is employed in the production of commodities. Capital generate crises because it constantly reduces the socially necessary labour time required for production of commodities. The rate of profit does not sink because the labourer is exploited any less, but because generally less labour is employed in proportion to the employed capital.

The real austerity project is to drive down wages and living standards in the west for decades, until they meet those of the middle class in China and India on the way up.

Structural adjustment and austerity programs of IMF and World Bank move from one developing country to the other, in its path destroying all remnants of functioning local structures, lowering wages, enfeebling labour rights and labour unions, opening these countries for imports and supplying local elites with pocket money they rarely invested back into the economy.

Roosevelt and Reagan took office when the previous regime of accumulation had exhausted itself, and the lineaments of a new one were to hand. In the thirties, there was no shortage of ideas in the Brains Trust or outside it — the Stockholm School, Keynes, Schacht — for how to overcome the Depression, even if it took time for the New Deal to make some use of them. In the eighties, a neo-liberal counter-attack — the Austrians, the Chicago School, Lucas — had long been in preparation, with an arsenal of prescriptions for dealing with stagflation to hand. Today, the regime of accumulation in place has fallen into disarray. But it is not yet in acute crisis; and subjectively, the landscape is barren of ideas that might adumbrate a new one. It is this underlying impasse which has produced a political scene at once closely and deeply divided.

## Neoliberalism is capitalism without working class opposition

The language of liberation is how capitalism masks it's actual process.

The key to capitalist discourse is its reliance on abstraction, invisibility, automation, and impersonal domination.

There's a human right for capital flight.

People accept the rule of capital not because they're duped by ideology and discourse, but because they correctly perceive no realistic alternative to its rule.

In the current phase of capitalism the accelerated mobility of capital favours societies that can cope most easily with inequality.

The paradigm of the neoliberal age is the indebted man.

As long as we believe that capitalism is bad, we are free to continue to participate in capitalist exchange.

Charity perpetuates the illusion that capitalism is just.

Capitalism, has evolved a new political ideology, welfare liberalism, which absolves individuals of moral responsibility and treats them as victims of social circumstance.

All of capitalism's structural pressures load the dice against collective action from below. They reinforce and encourage every tendency toward individualism and fragmentation, making successful collective organisation the exception to the norm.

Capitalism today doesn't care any more about symbolic signifiers, it just wants to make money.

Capitalism is not an economic system; it is not a social system; it is a way of organising nature.

Although capital brings into existence all the technical means to abolish labour, capital itself cannot realise this abolition, because labour is the sole source of surplus value for capital. Rather than abolishing labour, capital progressively renders labour superfluous to the production of material wealth.

The world economy is no longer growing. Capitalism, however, requires growth to prevent it being blown apart by the force of its inherent contradictions. If growth has halted, the expansion and centralisation of the productive forces comes to an end. With the end of growth, the centrifugal forces of disintegration are freely expressed, leading to the collapse of global institutions and states. We are not yet aware that this new normal has emerged in large part because we have been deluding ourselves that economic growth is the natural state of society.

Only in capitalism is exploitation naturalised, inscribed into the functioning of the economy, and not the result of extra-economic pressure and violence. This is why, with capitalism, we enjoy personal freedom and equality: there is no need for explicit social domination, since domination is already implicit in the structure of the production process.

Modern capitalist production arose in the first place, not because it was necessarily more efficient than other methods of organising work, but because it provided capitalists with greater profits and power.

Capitalism is an economic system that lives off labour, even though its continued development makes labour increasingly obsolete.

# APOPHTHEGM

The notion of a fully market socialist economy is incoherent. Just like the notion of a fully capitalist economy is incoherent. Every economy is going to be an ecosystem of heterogeneous, qualitatively distinct production and distribution mechanisms. The question is, "Which mechanisms dominate?" Not, "Which mechanisms take over everything?"

The neoliberal logic is that social change can be achieved through the power, and buying decisions, of dispersed, individual consumers.

Capitalism's shotgun marriage with democracy since 1945 is breaking up.

## Equality is not a point of principle, nor of opportunity

To focus on questions of distribution is a tendency that is harmful to sound economics.

A more equitable balance of power between capital and labour will have to emerge if the world is to enjoy the real benefits of trade.

Inequality is always in the context of ownership and decision-making, of expropriating the power of plutocrats, not just taxing them.

Relative mobility accounts for only a small portion of total mobility experienced by individuals across generations, whereas absolute or structural mobility accounts for most of it.

Meritocracy is predicated on the ridiculous and correspondingly cherished idea that individuals are born equal. Their success or failure must therefore come down to their own hard work and/or sense of personal responsibility. Statistics on economic success confirm that chances of succeeding have as much to do with privileged birth (or lack of it) as they ever did, so that meritocracy means those whose merit was once known as breeding will by and large run the show. A few low-born success stories help to disguise the persistence of things as they are, things as they were, things as they will be by-and-by.

The mobility mania and the cult of growth can be seen as an expression of the fear of aging that has become so intense in society.

As the middle classes and the post-Fordist generations shift their expectations for the good life away from public toward private consumption, those who, for lack of purchasing power, remain dependent on public provision are also affected. The attrition of the public sphere deprives them of their only effective means for making themselves heard, devaluing the political currency by which they might otherwise compensate for their lack of commercial currency. While those at the bottom of society have no place in commercial markets and their regime of resource allocation, they might extract benefits from potential allies more powerful than themselves in political coalitions in need of their support. Moreover, improving their lives might figure importantly in collective political visions of a good society, whereas markets can always do without them. In fact, the poor suffer in several ways from the de-politicisation of want satisfaction in affluent societies. Not only do the potentially reform-minded middle classes cease to take much interest or to place much confidence in collective projects: as they provide for themselves individually in the market, they become more resistant to paying taxes. Indeed with the declining social relevance of, and respect for, politics, tax resistance has increased everywhere, even in Scandinavia, and levels of taxation have fallen in all rich democracies.

## We live in a financial age, not a technological age

Financialisation is like a *Copernican revolution* in which business and society have reoriented their orbit around the financial sector.

If 1789 set history on the march toward subordination of the state to the democratic will of its citizens, 1971 was the year the state declared its independence from democracy. In 1971 the state demonstrated that it no longer needed to live off the meager resources it could raise through taxation and was thus free of all democratic control. Few people outside of the Modern Monetary Theory school realise exactly how much power the state has gained since 1971.

Developing new financial products is beneficial to the growth of capitalism. The plan to new financial-instrument futures need to be ambitious and should be greatly assisted by a regulatory stamp of approval.

The United Sates social security trust fund is prohibited from actively investing pension contributions in the open market, because of fears that its size would mean a step towards socialism.

It was not neoliberal ideology that broke the old system of financial regulations, but rather the contradictions that had emerged within that system.

Financialisation plays a vital role, both by integrating subordinate classes into a web of financial relations through private pensions, consumer credit and mortgages, and through facilitating consumer demand in an era of stagnating wages and limitations on the welfare state.

Financial markets are the most highly regulated markets, if regulation is measured by volume (number of pages) of rules, probably also if measured by extent of surveillance, and possibly even by vigour of enforcement.

Regulation controls competition and stabilises the market, while the welfare system socialises the human costs of capitalist production — rising unemployment, inadequate wage scales, inadequate insurance against sickness and old age — and helps to forestall more radical solutions.

Everybody hates inflation, but this attitude is deeply naive. Economists recognise that inflation has a number of positive effects. The first is that it makes debts easier to pay. The reason deflation is so dangerous is because it makes debts more onerous. The second is that inflation shifts consumption forward. If you think the refrigerator you desire will be more expensive next year, you shell out for it today. The third is that it increases entrepreneurs' profits. Businesses make the good before they sell it. Inflation means they make it for less and sell it for more. The group that gets really hammered by inflation is net creditors — those very few of us who lend more to others than they borrow from them, such as banks and the very very rich. It is a sign of their dominion over conventional wisdom that the rest of us have been taught to hate inflation, even if it actually would serve our interests.

When finance capital becomes globalised, while the state, which remains the only possible instrument through which the people could intervene on their own behalf, remains a nation state. The state accedes to the demands of finance capital, so that no matter whom the people elect, the same policies remain in place, as long as the country remains within the vortex of globalised finance.

## If you want to double your money, fold it and put it in your pocket

Money doesn't overcome poverty, it only redistributes it.

There is a commonplace and wrong assumption that money is the same as capital. This is not true: the wages of the worker is not her capital; it is merely money. Even in the hands of the capitalist money is only ideally capital. For money to become capital, it must be exchanged for labour power.

The point of a universal basic income is to give everybody the ability to say no. You have an expansive set of public goods, so that a significant part of everybody's consumption is not market based. People's standard of living doesn't depend simply on earnings; it depends upon the amenities that are publicly available plus your earnings. The combination of basic income plus public amenities means that you can live a decent life without engaging in capitalist relations of production.

Most supporters of universal basic income appear to believe that poverty, precarity and insecurity can be overcome by as simple a measure as handing out a pile of worthless currency to everyone in society.

If the central banks cannot raise interest rates on loaned capital above zero, why not try imposing a negative interest rate on the currency itself? We could have a technological means either of levying a negative interest rate on currency, or of breaking the constraint physical currency imposes on setting such a rate. We could levy a stamp tax on currency by randomly invalidating banknotes by serial number. A more radical proposal still would be to remove the zero lower bound constraint entirely by abolishing paper currency. This, has the added advantage of taxing illicit activities undertaken using paper currency, such as drug-dealing, at source. The problem with the zero lower bound is that credit becomes indistinguishable from currency. At the zero percent rate of interest there is no return on lent capital and the lender bears the additional risk of losing all or part of his lent capital. Once risk and overhead is factored into the loan, the real interest rate is negative. The lender would naturally see the advantage of sitting on his money capital than exposing it to a near 100% risk of losing money on the loan. The way around this problem is by imposing negative interest rate not on credit money, but on the currency itself. If a way could be found to force the holders of currency to pay interest on the currency in their banks accounts, wallets, pockets — and even in their mattresses — the distinction between credit money and currency could be forcibly imposed on society by the state despite a zero interest rate environment.

The state issues the treasuries not because it must borrow to operate, but because it must borrow to subsidise the rate of profit.

It is not that money, generated by the market, is appropriated by the state in order to finance public spending, but rather that the state, by accepting the money it mints as payment for taxes, gives it a guaranteed value that makes it useful for other kinds of transactions. The story of circulation always begins with the state.

Saying you want to displace the dollar as world reserve currency is essentially asking for an extinction level event: there is no way the US will ever concede this point short of nuclear holocaust.

## The worst crime against property is to have none

It is interesting that the word reform has come to mean privatisation.

Venture Capitalists are not funding Mother Teresa. They are funding imperial, will-to-power people who want to crush their competition. Companies can only have a big impact on the world if they get big.

The dirty secret of the VC trade is that the bottom three-quarters of venture firms didn't beat the Nasdaq for the past five years. The truth is that most VCs subsist entirely on fees, which they compound by raising a new fund every three years. Returns are kept hidden by non-disclosure agreements, and so VCs routinely overstate them, both to encourage investment and to attract entrepreneurs.

Wherever you have private property and money is the measure of all things, it is hardly ever possible for a commonwealth to be governed justly or happily.

The pleasure of consumerism is in shopping, not ownership or use. Ownership and use only demystify the goods in question, whereas shopping activates them, brings them to life in the imagination.

As the affluent lose interest in collective provision and instead turn to more expensive but, for them, affordable private alternatives, their exit from public in favour of private services accelerates the deterioration of the former and discourages their use even among those who depend upon them because they cannot afford the private alternatives.

# VIII
# Hysteria

## Free schools

In recent years, public education has been swamped by bad ideas and policies. Our leaders, most of whom were educated at elite universities and should know better, have turned this into a quest for higher scores on national tests. Evidence shows over and over again that standardised test scores are not the best way to measure and promote learning. Typically, what they measure is the demographic profile of schools.

Some of the most important things that matter in a quality education — critical thinking, intrinsic motivation, resilience, self-management, resourcefulness, and relationship skills — exist in the realms that can't be easily measured by statistical measures and computer algorithms, but they can be detected by teachers using human judgment. Business-inspired obsession with prioritising metrics in a complex world that deals with the development of individual minds has become the primary cause of mediocrity in schools.

It is puzzling that public officials have made national test scores the purpose of education. Aligned to this, are the punishments for not achieving higher national scores every year. A school that falls behind in the first year is required to provide evidence that it is on the right track — the turn around may involve firing the head teacher, or firing all or half of the staff, or doing something equally drastic. The ultimate goal, for those failing, is that to turn over to a private manager. There

## APOPHTHEGM

is, however, no evidence that this approach leads to better schools or higher test scores, but that does not matter.

In 2009, we had the best example of this autistic approach is the plan hatched by Democratic Mayor Cory Booker of Newark and Republican Governor Chris Christie of New Jersey to turn Newark into a United States model of education reform. Central to this hoped for miraculous transformation was a gift of $100 million by Facebook founder Mark Zuckerberg, matched by donations of another $100 million by other philanthropists who wanted to take part in a great adventure.

Newark's state schools had abysmal test scores and graduation rates and were generally considered a failure, despite high annual expenditures. Newark had one major attraction for the reformers: its schools have been under state control since 1995. The governor had total control of the district, its budget, and its leadership. The district had been taken over by the state because of poor academic performance and pervasive corruption. But in the next fifteen years, the state had not gotten better results than the regime it displaced. Newark's mayor since 2006, Cory Booker, wanted to uproot the school system and start over.

Booker and Christie agreed to create a plan for a radical transformation of the Newark state schools. The confidential draft of the plan that Booker sent to Christie proposed turning Newark into the charter school capital of the nation, weakening seniority and tenure, recruiting new teachers and principals from outside Newark, and, crucially, building sophisticated data and accountability systems.

In 2010, they persuaded Zuckerberg to get on board by advocating Newark was a city where he could demonstrate the success of his business-style school reforms. Booker believed that a great education would set every child on the road out of poverty, and he also believed that it would be impossible to do this in the Newark public schools because of their bureaucracy and systems of tenure and seniority. That's why he wanted to spend money turning the city into an all-charter district, without unions, where like-minded reformers could impose the correct reforms, like judging teachers by test scores, firing teachers at will, and hiring whomever they wanted. Zuckerberg, Booker, and

Christie announced the gift of $100 million on The Oprah Winfrey Show, to tumultuous applause. When Winfrey asked Zuckerberg why Newark, he responded, "I believe in these guys. We're setting up a $100 million challenge grant so that Mayor Booker and Governor Christie can have the flexibility they need to turn Newark into a symbol of educational excellence for the whole nation."

What Booker, Christie, and Zuckerberg set out to achieve in Newark had not been accomplished in modern times — turning a failing urban school district into one of universally high achievement. Booker believed that they knew what works. Zuckerberg's money would give him the chance to prove it.

They recruited a superintendent who had all the right qualifications and shared their ideas about reform — Cami Anderson. She had worked for Teach for America and Booker and Christie were particularly impressed with her toughness, a quality that was necessary in the job ahead of her. However, Anderson struggled to take control of the school district and impose reforms that outsiders loved and locals did not. The locals perceived her as an agent of the white philanthropists who had put up the money. She never won their confidence. In a city of deep poverty, she was making close to $300,000 a year, and hired pricey consultants to help her.

Despite this, Christie persuaded the Democratic legislature to weaken tenure. Anderson managed to negotiate a new contract with the teachers, which included performance pay and a new teacher evaluation system, as well as $31 million in back pay for teachers. She imposed a reorganisation of the school system that wiped out neighbourhood schools and reassigned students across the district. The residents' outrage boiled over as their children were assigned to distant schools instead of the one across the street. One father of five, accustomed to walking them to school every day, was furious when his children were assigned to five different schools in three different wards.

By the end of the story, Cory Booker had been elected to the United States Senate; Chris Christie is a perennial presidential hopeful; and, Anderson resigned. None of the reformers gave much thought to the majority of children who are not in charter schools, and not all of the charter schools are successful. Mark Zuckerberg watched his $100 million drained away by consultants, labour costs, and new charter schools. The Newark experiment did not produce a proof point or a replicable national model. Zuckerberg recognised a cautionary tale about the importance of working with local residents and not treating them and their children as objects to be moved around heedlessly by outsiders.

The lesson here for all future bureaucrats out there: improving education is not sufficient to save all children from lives of poverty and violence. As a society, we should be ashamed that so many children are immersed in poverty and violence every day of their lives.

## There is a growing belief that education should be painless, free of tension and conflict

Faith in the wonder-working power of education has proved to be one of the most durable components of liberal ideologies, easily assimilated by ideologies hostile to the rest of liberalism. Yet the democratisation of education has accomplished little to justify this faith. It has neither improved popular understanding of modern society, raised the quality of popular culture, not reduced the gap between wealth and poverty, which remains as wide as ever.

Mass education, which began as a promising attempt to democratise the higher culture of the privileged classes, has ended stupefying the privileged classes themselves.

The way we traditionally conceive of ignorance — as an absence of knowledge — leads us to think of education as its natural antidote. But education, even when done skillfully, can produce illusory confidence.

Learning should not be reduced to unstructured access and accumulation.

Being educated means being able to differentiate between what you know and what you don't. As it turns out, this simple ideal is extremely hard to achieve.

The dominant policy paradigm advocates education's vocational purpose: the goal is to ensure that young people can compete on a global economy.

People have lost the capacity for spontaneous feeling, even for anger. One of the essential aims of the educational process was to eliminate antagonism, to cultivate a commercialised friendliness.

The reforms of the progressive period gave rise to an unimaginative educational bureaucracy and a system of industrial recruitment that eventually undermined the ability of the school to serve as an agency of intellectual emancipation; but it as a long time before the effects of these changes became pervasive.

In education there is a steady dilution of intellectual standards in the name of relevance and other progressive slogans.

If an unfriendly foreign power attempted to impose on us the mediocre educational performance that exists today, we would view it as an act of war.

## We used to teach people to be free, now we teach them to work

The extension of formal schooling to groups formerly excluded from it is one of the most striking developments of modern history.

Here are the 10 purposes of the school reform programme: (1) form a labour force of cheerful robots; (2) eliminate critical thinking from schools; (3) generate immense profits for the education industry and information firms; (4) end teacher tenure, seize control of classrooms from professional educators, and break teachers' unions; (5) privatise public education through academisation and free schools; (6) facilitate private profits and financial speculation through control of government education funding; (7) merge education for large sections of the poor and racial minorities with the military and penal systems; (8) decrease the role of democracy in education while increasing the corporate role; (9) create databases with detailed biometrics on everyone, to be exploited by corporations; and (10) manage the population in what is a potentially fractious society divided by race and class.

## Universities are a sleepaway camp for overgrown children

Only hysteria produces new knowledge, in contrast to the University discourse, which simply reproduces it.

The tenure system is there to give professors the security to experiment with potentially dangerous ideas. Yet somehow the process of obtaining it reduces the proportion of the most perceptive and sophisticated human beings our society produces to a state in which they can't imagine what a dangerous idea would even look like.

The demand for more relevant courses has boiled down to a desire for an intellectually undemanding curriculum.

University English and foreign-language departments, once a citadel of high culture, no longer exist to evaluate literature in the interest of forming a canon of the very best writing; they prefer instead to diddle with theoretical distractions touching on what literature and movies and graphic novels and comic books and television shows tell about race, class, and gender.

Higher education has the task of solving society's concrete problems through the production of expert opinions. What disappears here is the true task of thinking: not only to offer solutions to problems posed by society, but to reflect on the very form of these problems; to discern a problem in the very way we perceive a problem.

It is crucial to link the push towards streamlining higher education — direct privatisation, links with business, and orienting education towards the production of expert knowledge — to the process of enclosing the commons of intellectual products, of privatising general intellect. This process is itself part of a global transformation in the mode of ideological interpellation.

## Wikipedia is less a new form of knowledge than a novel packaging of an old one

Without the ability to actively discriminate between good and bad, ugly and beautiful, useful and useless and, important and irrelevant we give away our inner capacity to decide and choose. We give away our capacity to forget and ensure that we can move forward convincingly. This is being intelligent. To accumulate all knowledge is not being intelligent — the mimic of a computer is not intelligence, it is information gathering. The reordering and the processing of this information is intelligence.

We live in an age where virtually no content is lost and virtually all content is shared. The sheer amount of information about every current idea makes those concepts difficult to contradict, particularly in a framework where public consensus has become the ultimate arbiter of validity. We're starting to behave as if we've reached the end of human knowledge. And while that notion is undoubtedly false, the sensation of certitude it generates is paralysing.

Both historically and today the real issue confronting society is how to give meaning to information — in other words, how to use information to create knowledge.

Because it's so easy to judge the idiocy of others, it may be sorely tempting to think this doesn't apply to you. But the problem of unrecognised ignorance is one that visits us all.

In many areas of life, incompetent people cannot recognise just how incompetent they are, a phenomenon that has come to be known as the Dunning-Kruger effect. Logic itself demands this lack of self-insight: for poor performers to recognise their ineptitude would require them to possess the very expertise they lack. To know how skilled or unskilled you are at using the rules of grammar, for instance, you must have a good working knowledge of those rules, an impossibility among the incompetent. Poor performers — and we are all poor performers at some things — fail to see the flaws in their thinking or the answers they lack.

# Rhopalic sentence

"I do not know where family doctors acquired illegibly perplexing handwriting; nevertheless, extraordinary pharmaceutical intellectuality, counterbalancing indecipherability, transcendentalizes intercommunications' incomprehensibleness." by Dmitri Borgmann in Language on Vacation: An Olio of Orthographical Oddities. This is a rhopalic sentence: A sentence or a line of poetry in which each word contains one letter or one syllable more than the previous word.

# IX
# Class

## Bullshit jobs

In the year 1930, John Maynard Keynes predicted that, by century's end, technology would have advanced sufficiently that countries like Great Britain or the United States would have achieved a 15-hour work week. There's every reason to believe he was right. In technological terms, we are quite capable of this. And yet it didn't happen. Instead, technology has been marshalled, if anything, to figure out ways to make us all work more. In order to achieve this, jobs have had to be created that are, effectively, pointless. Huge swathes of people, in Europe and North America in particular, spend their entire working lives performing tasks they secretly believe do not really need to be performed. The moral and spiritual damage that comes from this situation is profound. It is a scar across our collective soul. Yet virtually no one talks about it.

Why did Keynes' promised utopia never materialise? The standard line today is that he didn't figure in the massive increase in consumerism. Given the choice between less hours and more toys and pleasures, we've collectively chosen the latter. This presents a nice morality tale, but even a moment's reflection shows it can't really be true. Yes, we have witnessed the creation of an endless variety of new jobs and industries since the 1920s, but very few have anything to do with the production and distribution of sushi, iPhones, or fancy sneakers.

## APOPHTHEGM

So what are these new jobs, precisely? Over the course of the last century, the number of workers employed as domestic servants, in industry, and in the farm sector has collapsed dramatically. At the same time, professional, managerial, clerical, sales, and service workers tripled, growing from one-quarter to three-quarters of total employment. Productive jobs have, just as predicted, been largely automated away

But rather than allowing a massive reduction of working hours to free the world's population to pursue their own projects, pleasures, visions, and ideas, we have seen the ballooning of not even so much of the service sector as of the administrative sector, up to and including the creation of whole new industries like financial services or telemarketing, or the unprecedented expansion of sectors like corporate law, academic and health administration, human resources, and public relations. And these numbers do not even reflect on all those people whose job is to provide administrative, technical, or security support for these industries, or for that matter the whole host of ancillary industries (dog-washers, all-night pizza delivery) that only exist because everyone else is spending so much of their time working in all the other ones.

These are bullshit jobs. It's as if someone were out there making up pointless jobs just for the sake of keeping us all working. And here, precisely, lies the mystery. In capitalism, this is precisely what is not supposed to happen. Sure, in the old inefficient socialist states like the Soviet Union, where employment was considered both a right and a sacred duty, the system made up as many jobs as they had to. But, of course, this is the sort of very problem market competition is supposed to fix. According to economic theory, at least, the last thing a profit-seeking firm is going to do is shell out money to workers they don't really need to employ. Still, somehow, it happens.

While corporations may engage in ruthless downsizing, the layoffs and speed-ups invariably fall on that class of people who are actually making, moving, fixing and maintaining things; through some strange alchemy no one can quite explain, the number of salaried paper-pushers ultimately seems to expand, and more and more employees find themselves, not unlike Soviet workers actually, working 40 or even 50 hour weeks on paper, but effectively working 15 hours just as Keynes predicted, since the rest of their time is spent organising or attending motivational seminars, updating their Facebook profiles or downloading TV box-sets.

The answer clearly isn't economic: it's moral and political. The ruling class has figured out that a happy and productive population with free time on their hands is a mortal danger. And, on the other hand, the feeling that work is a moral value in itself, and that anyone not willing to submit themselves to some kind of intense work discipline for most of their waking hours deserves nothing, is extraordinarily convenient for them.

## The worst thing is to mix up work and happiness

The opposite of work is regarded as nothing more than consumption.

Labour is the activity that mediate humans and nature that transforms matter in a goal-directed manner and is a condition of social life.

Work ethic is the product of centuries of historical subordination.

Hard work constitutes a necessary but not sufficient cause of upward mobility.

Never have a job, because if you have a job someday someone will take it away from you and then you will be unprepared for your old age.

You have to have a high conception, not of what you are doing, but of what you may do one day: without that, there's no point in working.

The enjoyment of speed is a proxy for the enjoyment of work.

Nothing can make you believe we harbour nostalgia for factory work but a modern gym.

Employers want their employees to be authentic at work. The more work feels like home, the more and better work employees will do.

The 19th century cult of success placed surprisingly little emphasis on competition. It measured achievement not against the achievements

## APOPHTHEGM

of others, but against an abstract ideal of discipline and self-denial. At the turn of the century, however, preachments on success began to stress the will to win. The bureaucratisation of the corporate career changed the conditions of self-advancement; ambitious young men now had to compete with their peers for the attention and approval of their superiors.

A lot of what we call the sharing economy is really marginal, desperate middle class communities trying to sell whatever labour they have left over, or sell whatever items they own, to maintain their middle class lifestyle. That's not part of the pitch. That's not part of the empowerment rhetoric but, let's be honest, it's true.

If men have the talent to invent new machines that put men out of work, they have the talent to put those men back to work. It is a telling state of affairs that current political leaders steer away from this kind of discourse.

There is absolutely no convincing evidence of a causal relationship between dismantling labour-market rigidities and increasing wage dispersion on the one hand, and lowering unemployment on the other.

Labour is now used to plug what has not yet been mechanised.

Automation and unemployment are the future, regardless of any human intervention.

The state in the advanced countries literally has to create jobs to maintain full employment.

The unemployed do not hold down wages of the employed, but allow for the increase in employment during times of expansion.

The key determinant of employment rate is not wages; it is profits.

Marx's labour theory of value does not predict technological unemployment as might be assumed, but the actual expansion of wage employment in forms that produce neither value nor surplus value. From the standpoint of the process of accumulation as a whole, labour begins to lose its capacity to create value, it becomes empty. If this is correct, an hour of social labour no longer creates an hour of value as might be initially expected. On the one hand, as the social forces of production are developed by capital, an hour of social labour produces, perhaps, only 30, 20 or even five minutes of value; while, on the other hand, production of an hour of value requires two, three or even ten hours of actual expended social labour time. This is because, over time, the social labour day swells with labour that creates no value; labour that is materially superfluous to the production of commodities. The value-density of the social labour day falls.

## It is difficult to get a man to understand something, when his salary depends on his not understanding it

Freedom is not the freedom to accumulate, but the fact that we have no need to accumulate.

De-unionisation is estimated to cost black American men $50 a week.

There are times when the regulatory state is the only viable way to address an immediate political problem (for example, the 2008 financial crisis). But, it's important to remember these kinds of solutions are inadequate over the long haul, because they do not change the underlying balance of power in society. And, that balance is the key to democracy. This is why unions are so important to a democratic society: They are one of the few means available for workers to express their own preferences without the distorting filter of markets or market-oriented bureaucracies.

Consumer was formerly known as the worker. The rebranding reflects a fundamental shift in the role of the state. The rights of the consumer as final buyer of labour must be defended against his or her own claims as a seller of labour. So that when competition law works properly the labour-seller should earn and consume less.

While capitalistic accumulation reduces the labour time technically required for production of commodities, and thus lays the material basis for a general reduction of social labour time for the social producers, it leads not to a shortening of hours of labour, nor even technological unemployment, but to a new category of labour time, superfluous labour time. This reflects the contradiction: as determined by the old relations of production it remains labour time; as judged in terms of the potential of the new forces of production it is, in its old determination, superfluous.

The workers' movement was internationalist, as it was also opposed to property, to the state, to the family, to the Church, to the army, to corrective justice, and so on in the revolutionary manner. The tone of the most humdrum trade union meeting then would astonish the boldest ultra-left vanguard groupuscule today. The movement was destroyed by social democracy and Stalinism, precisely because they have abandoned the idea of communism and created two versions of planned state capitalism, quite egalitarian and plebeian, and have weakened or obliterated altogether the political class rule of the old bourgeoisie, but did not (or could not do) anything about the separation of the means of production (means of subsistence) from the producers. Commodity production and wage labor continued unabated.

The labour time required for production of surplus value has no direct relation to the labour time required for realising this surplus value as profit.

## The working class, for all its potentials as an actor, stumbles aimlessly on

Contemporary protest works because it creates a sense that we are doing something and it is reinforced when a minor battle is actually won.

The essentially affective, gestural, and experimental politics of movements such as Occupy, are a retreat from the tradition of serious militant politics, to something like politics-as-drug-experience. Whatever their problems with the psychodynamics of such actions, localism and small scale, prefigurative politics are simply inadequate to challenging the ideological dominance of neoliberalism — they are out of step with the actualities of the global capitalist system.

Contestation has always been an essential act. Saints, hermits and intellectuals, those few who have made history, are the ones who have said no, not the courtesans and Cardinals' assistants. So as to be meaningful, contestation must be large, major and total, absurd and not in a good sense. It cannot merely be on this or that point.

The capitalist maintains his rights as a purchaser when he tries to make the working day as long as possible. On the other hand, the labourer maintains his right as seller when he wishes to reduce the working day to one of definite normal duration. There is here therefore an antinomy, of right against right, both equally bearing the seal of the law of exchange. Between equal rights force decides.

There's no illegal strike, just an unsuccessful one.

No one is in the streets demanding an immediate end to wage slavery and a society founded on the principle of to each according to their need. Indeed, people aren't even in the streets demanding a Keynesian program of full employment and a higher minimum wage.

Dreams are an investment — they're expensive and involve a lot of risk that working class people can't in many ways afford. Poor people aren't allowed to pursue their dreams.

For the period of time a worker is free to make a contract he is also forced to do so.

Only in the factory is the worker of today a real proletarian. Outside the factory he is a petty bourgeois, involved in a petty bourgeois milieu and middle class habits of life, dominated by petty bourgeois ideology.

The working class cannot simply lay hold of the readymade state machinery, and wield it for its own purposes.

The working class is the only class that can produce a classless society because it is in its interest to do so.

The professional managerial class monopoly on progressive left politics is a development in class conflict that had profound effects on the rise of neoliberalism and globalisation. While this class emerged as an enemy or at least an antagonist of capital during the early decades of the 20th century, its political neutrality has become increasingly complicit with the status quo of income inequality. In order to differentiate itself culturally from the working classes and the interests of finance capital, it draws upon the sentimental and melodramatic innovations of its forebears of the 18th century. Suffering and victimisation become its calling cards: a precious and esoteric language of difference and tolerance supplant an analysis of contradiction and solidarity. It focuses on hegemonic cultural politics and self-improvement and the transformation of everyday life.

## A fully hegemonic class rules through liberal institution

Class is different from other identities: it's invisible, nuanced, relative, and people generally don't like to talk about it.

The state is not the cause of social divisions, but a product of those social divisions. As long as society remains divided by classes, classes will give rise to states that, essentially, are only dictatorships of one class over another.

The race question is subsidiary to the class question in politics, and to think of imperialism in terms of race is disastrous. There is a subordination of race to class.

As conversation takes on the quality of confession, class consciousness declines; people perceive their social position as a reflection of their own abilities and blame themselves for the injustices inflicted on them. Politics degenerates into a struggle not for a social change but for self-realisation.

The ruling class can deal with any one individual or any small group; it's only masses that can stand in their way.

The language of money always speaks with an accent and, normally an upper class one.

Means-tested puts an end to the epidemic of poor people buying convertibles and caviar with welfare checks and food stamps.

The yellow vests movement marks the failure of a project born in the late 1980s and later led by the evangelists of social liberalism, to create a centrist republic in France that would end ideological upheavals by pushing the working class out of public debate and political institutions.

In today's English, *pig* refers to the animals with which farmers deal, while *pork* is the meat we consume. The class dimension is clear here: *pig* is the old Saxon word, since Saxons were the underprivileged farmers, while *pork* comes from the French porque, used by the privileged Norman conquerors who mostly consumed the pigs raised by farmers. This duality signals the gap that separates production from consumption.

## The middle class are in fact the real perverts of modernity

Much of what is known as the middle class is because it dresses up to go to work.

The conflict between capital and labour is not going to be solved by the bourgeoisie.

The absence of social theory serves to perpetuate the bourgeois social order.

The human rights discourse is a weapon of the bourgeoisie that emerged during the birth capitalism which naturalises their own priorities and extends them into universal discourse onto the working classes in order to achieve their subjugation.

The capitalist class owes its longevity in power by dividing itself into progressive bourgeoisie and republican bourgeoisie, clerical bourgeoisie and free-thinking bourgeoisie. This way that a defeated faction can always be replaced in power by another faction from the same class.

The ultimate bourgeois virtue is thrift, and the ultimate working class virtue is solidarity.

The bourgeois do not succeed entirely in being feudal; they create their own nobility through their labour.

## Nothing succeeds like the appearance of success

I am so good at managing people that a man I once fired later thanked me for the unexpected opportunity to self-actualise, a happy occurrence because there's nothing I detest more than people who play the victim.

I want the people working for me to be worse off than I am, not better. That's the reason I pay you so well. I want to see you right on the verge. I want it right out in the open. I want to be able to hear it in the stuttering, flustered, tongue-tied voice. Don't trust me. I don't trust flattery, loyalty, and sociability. I don't trust deference, respect, and cooperation. I trust fear.

Professional advancement had come to depend less on craftsmanship or loyalty to the firm than on visibility, momentum, personal charm, and impression management.

If it is true that some degree of talent is necessary to be successful in life, almost never the most talented people reach the highest peaks of success, being overtaken by mediocre but sensibly luckier individuals.

Modern leadership is either the act of walking in front of a group of people that already know where they are going. Or, taking people to a place they don't want to go.

## Only those who dare to fail greatly can ever achieve greatly

Modern games and sports had been ruined by a fatal shift toward over-seriousness.

Games enlist skill and intelligence, the utmost concentration of purpose, on behalf of activities utterly useless, to the wealth of comfort of the community, or to its physical survival.

The uselessness of games makes them offensive to social reformers, improvers of public morals, of functionalist critics of society.

Wrestling is the only sport which gives us an externalised image of torture.

Football used to be more of a sport, and less a subset of the entertainment industry.

If you want to enjoy something run 100 metres. If you want to experience something, run a marathon.

Isiah Thomas: When Larry Bird makes a great play, it's due to his thinking, and his work habits. It's all planned out by him. It's not the case for blacks. All we do is run and jump. We never practise or give a thought to how we play. It's like I came dribbling out of my mother's womb.

Everything testifies to the invasion of play by the rhetoric of achievement.

# X
# Laika

## Vulcan

Pierre-Simon Laplace had gone to his grave in 1827 convinced that he had shown that the solar system as a whole could be rendered intelligible, its motions accounted for by Newtonian gravitation as expressed within mathematical models — the theory of the planets. Properly employed, those models could describe the motions of the physical system explicitly, accurately, and indefinitely into the future. If there was some work left to do, new methods to be explored, more observations to be considered, discoveries within the system (like the newly discovered minor planets, asteroids and comets), the basic picture seemed sound.

There were, though, more anomalies than the edifice of his *Celestial Mechanics* book acknowledged. Some of the theories of the planets were proving a bit less settled than Laplace had believed, and some, like Mercury's, were obviously inadequate, unable to predict the planet's behaviour with remotely acceptable precision. Despite such problems, no researcher had yet returned to the whole of Laplace's program. Several astronomers in France and elsewhere worked on individual questions in planetary dynamics, but none were trying to resolve the system as a whole, to go from a theory of any given planet to one of the solar system, top to bottom.

Enter Urbain Jean Joseph Le Verrier, a tobacco engineer at the École

## APOPHTHEGM

Polytechnique. Over his first two years at the Polytechnique, Le Verrier surveyed the whole field of solar system dynamics, beginning to suspect that seemingly minor gravitational interactions might matter more than his predecessors had believed — that over time they produce effects that would be noticeable. He seized the opportunity, setting himself as his first major project the goal of recalculating at higher mathematical resolution the motions of the four inner planets — Mercury, Venus, Earth, and Mars. It took him just two years, a phenomenal pace given that he had started from zero as a mathematical astronomer.

Le Verrier presented his results to the French Academy of Sciences in 1839. He came to one striking conclusion: when you take one more term into consideration than prior calculations had attempted, it becomes impossible to say for certain whether or not the orbit of the inner planets would remain stable over the very long haul. Neither he nor anyone else knew how to find a complete solution to the equations that could confirm whether Mercury, Venus, Mars — and Earth — would remain forever on their present tracks.

Laplace had concluded from his studies of Jupiter and Saturn that the stability of the solar system was proved; here was a young man just two years into the field suggesting otherwise.

This was still preliminary work, but it managed to hook him on celestial mechanics as a life project — and for his next major task, he set himself a problem that no prior researcher had been able to solve: Mercury.

Over the preceding decade, advances in instruments and technique made it possible to follow Mercury with a previously unattainable accuracy. With this new technology and new data, Le Verrier was able to construct a better picture of the way Venus influenced Mercury's orbit as the two planets moved from one configuration to another. That, in turn, led him to a new estimate of Mercury's mass, with his answer falling within a few percentage points of the modern value.

These were satisfying outcomes — filling in some of the more elusive details of one corner of the solar system. But Le Verrier really wanted a complete account of Mercury, a system of equations encompassing the full range of gravitational tugs that affect its orbit, which can be used to identify planetary positions past and future. Observations constrain such models: any solution to a model's equations has to at least reproduce what observers already know about a planet's orbit. More data meant more constraint, and hence a more accurate set of predictions about where the planet would go next.

The final exam for Le Verrier's first version of such a theory for Mercury came in 1845, its next scheduled transit of the sun. An astronomer at the eyepiece of the telescope trained on the sun saw the dark break which the black body of the planet made on the bright disk of the sun. Against Le Verrier's prediction, Mercury was sixteen seconds late.

This was an impressive result — better by far than any previous published schedule for Mercury. But it wasn't good enough. That sixteen-second error, small as it seemed, still meant that Le Verrier had Mercury in transit across the face of the sun in 2006 missed something that kept the real Mercury out of sync with his abstract, theoretical planet. Le Verrier had planned to publish his calculation following the transit. Instead, he pulled the manuscript and let the problem lie for a time. Mercury would have to wait quite a while, as it turned out, for almost immediately he found himself conscripted into a new confrontation.

Uranus was the troublemaker, and had been for decades. After Herschel's serendipitous discovery of the new planet, astronomers swiftly realised that others had seen it before, thinking it a star. In 1690, John Flamsteed, the first Astronomer Royal and Newton's collaborator placed it on one of his sky maps as the star 34 Tauri. Dozens of other missed-chance observations turned up in observers' records, until in 1821, one of Laplace's students at the Bureau, Alexis Bouvard, combined those historical sightings with the systematic searches that had followed Herschel's news to create a new table for Uranus, one supposed to confirm that it obeyed the same Newtonian laws that governed its planetary kin.

He failed. When he attempted to construct a theory of Uranus that could generate by calculation the positions observers had recorded since Herschel's night of discovery, he couldn't make the numbers work. Anything he tried that agreed with observations made since 1781 didn't line up with the rediscovered positions that had been misidentified as stars before that date. Even worse, when he focused only on the more recent, post-Herschel record, it quickly became clear that the planet was again wandering off course — reality and calculation diverged.

In the abstract, such uncooperative behaviour might point to a very deep problem: if all the gravitational influences on Uranus had been accounted for, the failure to predict its motion would demand a re-examination of the theory behind such analysis. That is: it could threaten the foundations of Newton's laws themselves. One researcher, the German astronomer Friedrich Wilhelm Bessel, wondered, if perhaps, Newton's gravitational constant itself might vary with distance.

Such thoughts were thinkable, but horrifying. The tides obeyed its rules; comets were brought to order under its provisions; cannonballs flew on courses perfectly described and explained by the exquisite logic of the *Principia*. Better, by far, would be any explanation that captured this seeming anomaly within a Newtonian framework.

It seemed that, Alexis Bouvard was the first to come up with a way to do so. In 1845, his nephew, Eugène Bouvard, reported to the Académie his own, unsuccessful attempt to bring Uranus's track to mathematical order. Following his uncle, he tried to resolve modern observations with older ones. He failed, and admitted as much. But still, he told his learned audience there was a way out, one his uncle had glimpsed two decades earlier. It was not the one Laplace had used to resolve the Jupiter-Saturn mystery. That involved improving the mathematical technique with which he attempted to describe the world out there. Rather, the older Bouvard reasoned, if all the known behaviours of the solar system could not account for the last residue of error — and crucially, if you maintained your faith in Newton — then the only remaining possibility was that something unknown would resolve the matter. Bouvard reminded his readers that if they imagined Uranus had remained undiscovered, then meticulous attention to Saturn would reveal the influence of some more distant unseen celestial body. However, he admitted that it was entirely plausible that another planet was perturbing Uranus.

One obvious difficulty was that Uranus was too damn slow. Its eighty-eight-(Earth-)year-long period meant that systematic observations since Herschel had followed roughly half of a single journey around the sun.

Le Verrier thought this wouldn't be a problem. Late in the summer of 1845, François Arago, the director of the Paris Observatory, convinced Le Verrier to look at the errors within the theory of Uranus. Le Verrier began by identifying several errors in the older Bouvard's sums. Those mistakes did not eliminate the unexplained wobbles in Uranus's orbit, so Le Verrier instead recalculated the planet's tables to define those anomalies as precisely as possible. With the intellectual ground thus cleared, he turned into a detective, seeking the as-yet-unidentified perpetrator that could have led Uranus astray.

As a good police procedural would have it, he soldiered on, examining — and eliminating — as many suspects as he could. Perhaps there was something about the space out by Uranus, some resisting stuff (an ether) that affected its motion. Was there a giant moon orbiting Uranus, tugging it off course? Might some stray object, a comet, perhaps, have collided with Uranus, literally knocking it from its appointed round? Le Verrier even paused on the fraught possibility that Newton's law of gravitation might need modification. Last: was there some as-yet-undiscovered object, another planet, whose gravitational influence could account for the discrepancies between Uranus's theoretically predicted and the observed track?

Le Verrier quickly rejected the first potential candidates. He agreed with virtually every professional astronomer in thinking that modifying or rejecting Newtonian gravitation would be a final, desperate resort. Which meant that after several months of thinking about the problem, he was back to his prime suspect: an as-yet-undiscovered trans-Uranian planet.

With that, his task was sharply defined: once all the known sources of

## APOPHTHEGM

gravitational influence were accounted for, what were the properties — mass, distance, finer details of its orbit — of the object that could account for the remaining anomalies in the motion of Uranus? In that form, the problem resolved down to a conventional problem in celestial mechanics, establishing and then solving a system of equations that described each of the components of the hypothetical planet's motion.

Le Verrier first set up his calculation with thirteen unknowns — too many for someone with even his gifts to solve in any timely manner. So he simplified his assumptions. He argued that there had to be a sweet spot for at least some of the orbital parameters of the missing planet. It couldn't be too close to Uranus, for then its effects would have been too obvious. It couldn't be terribly far away, as that would imply a large enough mass to affect Saturn as well, and no such influence had been detected. He simply guessed that its orbit wouldn't be too sharply angled to the plane of the rest of the planets. He constructed a few more such arguments to fill in some of the gaps in the observational data from Uranus, which left him with a system of equations with just nine unknowns.

Calculating a unique solution within that model — one that would give him a prediction of the mass and position for the planet — proved almost ludicrously laborious. Being clever helped, as when he came up with a way to transform some of the essentially intractable nonlinear equations in the model into a larger set of linear expressions. That made the calculation possible, but at the cost of a horrific amount of grunt work to crank through the much greater number of steps the new approach required.

On August 31, 1846, Le Verrier concluded that if anyone happened to have time to spare on a good telescope, they should find a planet beyond the orbit of Uranus at a distance of about 36 astronomical units, visible about five degrees east of $\varnothing$ Capricorn — a fairly bright star within the Capricorn constellation. Its mass, Le Verrier declared, would be about thirty-six times that of Earth, and to the telescope-aided eye, it would reveal itself not as a point (like a star), but as a clearly discernible disk, 3.3 arcseconds in diameter.

On the night of September 23, 1846, in Berlin, watchers at the Royal Observatory spotted a previously unmapped star. This visible circle can mean just one thing: the watchers has just become the first men to see a previously undiscovered planet, one that would come to be called Neptune, just about exactly where Urbain-Jean-Joseph Le Verrier told them to look.

This was the climax of what was almost immediately understood to be the popular triumph of Newtonian science. The discovery of Neptune — driven by the mathematical interpretation of fundamental laws, so exactly as to reveal itself within hours of the start of the search — was recognised at once as both a stunning display of individual genius and a triumph for a whole way of knowing the world. This transformed the discovery of Neptune as a celebration of science as a whole. Le Verrier had confronted an uncomfortable fact, and then subjected it to theory, the theory, Newton's system of the world, to risk a prediction that then proved true. If ever there was a demonstration of how science is supposed to advance, here it was.

It wasn't until 1859, sixteen years after his first attempt, that Le Verrier found himself free to return to the problem of Mercury. He was forty-eight years old, at the height of both his fame and, by all witness testimony, his mathematical powers. He had the resources of the Paris Observatory at his disposal. Mercury's theory should have been a straightforward task.

It was and it wasn't. The older Le Verrier had one absolute advantage over his younger self: better data. He re-examined the information he had used in 1843 — measurements of Mercury's motion made at the Observatory itself. To that he added the best observations it was possible to make at the current state of astronomical technology: transits, with high-quality records for Mercury extending back to 1697. With a good clock and an accurate fix on where on earth the event was being viewed, timing a planet's entry or exit from a transit ranked among the most precise measurements available to astronomers.

Le Verrier launched his assault following his usual plan. First he mapped out Mercury's actual orbit with all of its components of motion as described by the empirical data: direct measurements of

## APOPHTHEGM

Mercury's behaviour. Next came calculation: what do Newton's laws predict for Mercury, given all the known gravitational contributions of the planets as well as the sun? Any discrepancies between the empirical picture and the theoretical one must then be explained. If there were none, then the theory of the planet was complete, and the model of the solar system would be one step closer to being done.

But there was a leftover result. It was a small number, but the gap between theory and the data was greater than estimates of observational errors could explain, which meant the problem was real. That settled one matter: it strongly suggested that Mercury's difficulties almost certainly lay not with flaws in Le Verrier's analysis, but rather in something unknown out there in space.

The particular anomaly he found is called the precession of the perihelion of Mercury's orbit. In the squashed circle of an elliptical orbit, the point at which a planet comes closest to its star is called its perihelion. In an idealised two-body system, that orbit is stable and the perihelion remains fixed, always coming at the same point in the annual cycle. Once you add more planets, though, that constancy evaporates. In such a system, if you were to map each year's track onto a single sheet of paper, you would over time draw a kind of flower petal, with each oval just slightly shifted. The perihelion (and its opposite number, the aphelion, or most distant point in the orbit) would move around the sun. When that shift comes in the direction that the planet moves in its annual journey, the perihelion is said to advance. A circular (or elliptical) orbit covers 360 degrees, with each degree divided up into sixty minutes of arc; and, each minute into sixty arcseconds. Le Verrier's analysis told him that this was happening to Mercury: its perihelion advances at a rate of 565 arcseconds every hundred years.

Next came a round of celestial bookkeeping: how much of that total could be explained by the influence of the other planets on Mercury. Venus, as Mercury's neighbour, proved to be doing most of the work. Le Verrier's sums revealed that it accounted for almost exactly half of the precession, 280.6 seconds of arc per century. Jupiter provided another 152.6 to the total, Earth 83.6, with the rest causing scraps of motion. The total: 526.7 arcseconds per century. An error of just 38 arcseconds per century.

Tiny, but the excess perihelion advance of Mercury retained one crucial property: it wasn't zero. Le Verrier knew what such unreconciled motion must mean. If Mercury moved where no known mass existed to push it, then there was some imperfection of our knowledge waiting to be repaired.

Le Verrier arrived at the obvious conclusion: a planet, or a group of smaller planets circling in the vicinity of Mercury's orbit, would be capable of producing the anomalous perturbation felt by the latter planet. According to this hypothesis, the mass sought should exist inside the orbit of Mercury. By no later than February 1860, the solar system's newest planet knew its name: Vulcan.

Matters soon grew more complicated, though. Reports of sightings arrived, some from reputable observers, others from unknowns. To those for whom the logical necessity of Vulcan was overwhelming, this spray of messages was comforting, not proof in and of itself, but an ongoing accumulation of information building on an already established pattern. The lack of a pure Neptune moment must have been frustrating, but given the inherent difficulty of the problem, such momentary glimpses gained significance each time another letter from some sincere and precise stranger reached Paris. But despite a growing heap of such hopeful wisps, Vulcan remained almost maliciously elusive when confronted by a systematic search.

A way out was obvious to the more mathematically sophisticated Vulcan hunters. People simply could have gotten their sums wrong. There were enough imprecise assumptions about the elements of a putative Vulcan's orbit so that calculations for transits could just be wrong. Princeton's Stephen Alexander told his fellow members of the National Academy of Sciences that he had reworked Vulcan's elements to arrive at the conclusion that there should be a planet or group of planets at a distance of about twenty-one million miles from the sun, and with a period of 34 days and 16 hours. In other words: we may have been looking in the wrong places, or at the wrong times. Vulcan could be elusive, but not absent.

# APOPHTHEGM

That claim seemed to be confirmed when Heinrich Weber sent word from northeast China that he had seen a dark circular shape transit the sun on April 4, 1876. Sunspot expert and Vulcan devotee Rupert Wolf passed word of his colleague's sighting on to Paris.

However, Le Verrier remained doubtful and returned to the contemplation of Vulcan. He began a comprehensive re-examination of everything that might bear upon its existence. Starting with yet another catalogue of claimed sightings dating back to 1820, he identified five observations spread from 1802 to 1862 that seemed to him most likely to represent repeat glimpses of a single planet. That allowed him to construct a new theory for the planet, complete with the prediction: a transit that could perhaps be observed on October 2nd or 3rd.

But, Vulcan did not cross the face of the sun in early October. Additionally, Weber's revelation from China was debunked: two photographs made at the Greenwich Observatory clearly revealed his Vulcan to be just another sunspot. Le Verrier said nothing more in public about Vulcan. He had turned sixty-six on March 11, and he was tired to the bone. As the year advanced, he found he couldn't drag himself to the weekly meetings of the Académie, nor to his daily post at the Observatory. Time off seemed to help — he returned to his desk in August — but fatigue masked his real trouble: liver cancer.

Le Verrier left the solar system larger than he found it — one both better and less completely understood. Of Vulcan itself, though — surely, given all the fully satisfactory explanations for the behaviour of every other astronomical object derived from the Newtonian synthesis, the fault, it seemed so nearly certain, must lie not in the stars, but in some human failure to crack this one particular mystery.

Vulcan itself dwindled into a mostly forgotten embarrassment, the physical sciences' crazy uncle in the attic. Mercury's perihelion still moved. The gap between fact and explanation remained.

That would change — but only after a young man in Switzerland started to think about something else entirely, nothing to do with any confrontation between a planet and an idea. One way we would now reframe this problem is to ask how fast gravity travels from here to there, from the sun, say, to Earth.

In November 18, 1915, Einstein revealed how his own relativity theory agreed completely with the observations. Decades of attempts to save the Newtonian worldview were at an end. Vulcan was gone, dead, utterly unnecessary. No chunk of matter was required to explain Mercury's track, no undiscovered planet, no asteroid belt, no dust, no bulging solar belly, nothing at all — except this new, radical conception of gravity. The sun with its great mass creates its dent in space-time. Mercury, so firmly embraced by our star's gravitational field, lies deep within that solar gravity well. Like all objects navigating space-time, Mercury's motion follows that warping, four-dimensional curve. Einstein finally captured in all the abstract majesty of his mathematics, the orbit of the innermost planet precesses away from the Newtonian ideal. Einstein's pen destroyed Vulcan — and reimagined the cosmos.

## Extraordinary claims require extraordinary evidence

The scientists' account of nature reflects and constitutes society and culture.

A widespread revolt against reason is as much a feature of our world as our faith in science and technology.

Science has not displaced religion, as so many people once expected. Both seem to flourish side by side, often in grotesquely exaggerated form.

The origin and evolution of life is prima facie highly implausible that life as we know it is the result of a sequence of physical accidents, together with the mechanism of natural selection. It flies in the face of common sense.

Something is not necessarily either true or false; it can be both true and false.

Our world obeys rules still alien to our imagination.

In the 1930s, Karl Popper drew a line between science and non-sci-

## APOPHTHEGM

ence in comparing the work of Albert Einstein with that of Sigmund Freud. Einstein's theory of general relativity, which cast the force of gravity as curves in space and time, made risky predictions — ones that, if they hadn't succeeded so brilliantly, would have failed miserably, falsifying the theory. But Freudian psychoanalysis was slippery: any fault of your mother's could be worked into your diagnosis. The theory wasn't falsifiable, and so, Popper decided, it wasn't science.

The weight of evidence for an extraordinary claim must be proportioned to its strangeness.

The worst analytical crimes have been committed in the name of some kind of simplicity.

We have been Darwinists about the animal kingdom but Creationists about the human head.

Sturgeon's law: 90% of everything is crap. So, 90% of experiments in molecular biology, 90% of poetry, 90% of philosophy books, 90% of peer-reviewed articles in mathematics are crap. A good moral to draw from this observation is that when you want to criticise a field, a genre, a discipline, an art form, don't waste your time and ours hooting at the crap. In order not to waste your time and try your patience, make sure you concentrate on the best stuff you can find, the flagship examples extolled by the leaders of the field, the prize-winning entries, not the dregs.

The number of truly great scientists has been progressively drowned out by the much more rapidly increasing number of merely competent ones.

If peer review is good at anything, it appears to be keeping unpopular ideas from being published.

We need to break the secrecy around professional and expert knowledge. Challenge the division between scientific knowledge and everyday practice, between manual and intellectual work. We are probably already too conditioned by the system to be sure whether our projects are a real innovation or a mere management reform.

The case against science is straightforward: much of the scientific literature, perhaps half, may simply be untrue. Afflicted by studies with small sample sizes, tiny effects, invalid exploratory analyses, and flagrant conflicts of interest, together with an obsession for pursuing fashionable trends of dubious importance, science has taken a turn towards darkness.

We lionize the scientist as head-in-the-clouds genius (the Einstein hero) and the inventor as misfit-in-the-garage genius (the Steve Jobs or Bill Gates hero). The discomfiting reality, however, is that much of today's technological world exists because of Pentagon's role in catalysing and steering science and technology. This was industrial policy, and it worked because it brought all of the players in the innovation game together, disciplined them by providing strategic, long-term focus for their activities, and shielded them from the market rationality that would have doomed every crazy, over-expensive idea that today makes the world go round.

DNA (deoxyribonucleic acid) is the main component of our genetic material. It is formed by combining four parts: A, C, G and T (adenine, cytosine, guanine and thymine), called bases of DNA combine in thousands of possible sequences to provide the genetic variability that enables the wealth of aspects and functions of living beings. In the early 80s, to these four classic bases of DNA was added a fifth: the methylcytosine (mC) derived from cytosine. And it was in the late 90's when mC was recognised as the main cause of epigenetic mechanisms: it is able to switch genes on or off depending on the physiological needs of each tissue. In recent years, interest in this fifth DNA base has increased by showing that alterations in the methylcytosine contribute to the development of many human diseases, including cancer. Now, there is the possible existence of a sixth DNA base, the methyl-adenine (mA), which also help determine the epigenome and would therefore be key in the life of the cells.

Chomsky remarked that every human language can be acquired by any human being. Universal grammar must be a species-specific characteristic of the human race, biologically encoded, genetically transmitted.

## APOPHTHEGM

Chang and Eng Bunker were conjoined twin brothers, born on May 11, 1811 in Siam (now Thailand). Their condition and birthplace became the basis for the term Siamese twins.

Time passes faster in the mountains than it does at sea level.

## All Watched Over By Machines Of Loving Grace

I like to think (and
the sooner the better!)
of a cybernetic meadow
where mammals and computers
live together in mutually
programming harmony
like pure water
touching clear sky.

I like to think
(right now, please!)
of a cybernetic forest
filled with pines and electronics
where deer stroll peacefully
past computers
as if they were flowers
with spinning blossoms.

I like to think
(it has to be!)
of a cybernetic ecology
where we are free of our labors
and joined back to nature,
returned to our mammal
brothers and sisters,
and all watched over
by machines of loving grace.

## There is nothing sacred about technology

If you are worried that artificial intelligence will eclipse human intelligence, you may be falsely assuming that intelligence implies a will to power.

In a false society, technology develops wrongly.

The financial crisis shifted most of the mendacity from the banking industry to the tech sector.

Silicon valley is the logical culmination of the fetishisation of knowledge and information.

Treating the world as software promotes fantasies of control.

We are living in a simulation and that's the ultimate loss of control. Instead of writing the software, we are the software.

The difficulty with technology is not that it enhances our lives. It does. Rather, it's that it radically prescribes the life it enhances in the process.

Modern technology encapsulates the view of man as an all-powerful subjectum, a tyrant who orders, manipulates, and controls the things of the world.

The machine is one of the great emancipatory developments in the history of humankind. The machine can relieve workers of needless toil; it can be a tool which frees human labour, lengthens and broadens the life of the simplest man.

Whether it is colonising Mars or finding a parking spot in San Francisco, the tech industry promises to tackle humanity's greatest challenges.

Telephone is an invention of the devil which abrogates some of the advantages of making a disagreeable person keep his distance.

The telephone destroyed the art of correspondence, and in the process diminished the moral stature of attempts at rational systematization;

## APOPHTHEGM

email has not restored it.

New technologies of permanent connectivity put the world at the disposal of the body, dispensing it from belonging, being represented, debating or voting.

### You cannot monetize the network

We used to search for intelligent life in the universe, now we are reduced to search for it on the Internet.

The utopian Internet cant about flattened, decentralised power networks jibes nicely with one of the most enduring middle-class romantic dreams that we have inherited from the hippies and never quite shaken off: the dream of leaderless, horizontally-structured utopias in which power itself dissolves along with the old oppressive vertical hierarchies.

The state exerts no control of the Internet; it leaves this to corporations.

The internet stands to replicate the worst aspects of television: passivity, mediocrity, a plurality of superficial choice with the same indistinguishable affect.

The economic basis of the Internet is surveillance.

Facebook revolution is self-surveillance from below.

Facebook will have a hard time being hyper-subjective (tailoring content to the revealed preferences of its users) and hyper-objective (filtering its entire ecosystem for accuracy as though accuracy doesn't require a standpoint). It would be better for the world if Facebook did not pretend it was capable of doing both.

The Like button was created to put Facebook users to work at producing Facebook's programming.

Internet obfuscation permits gestures of independence that feel satisfying, without changing the actual conditions of domination.

Only a meta-narrative about technology that's alive today which is similar to the metanarrative of the End of History, the foundation of the liberal consensus in America and much of Europe today. The Internet narrative challenges any alternative conceptualisations of historical change. We have this meta-story of something called the Internet coming around and disrupting everything, and then its smaller, bullshit-oriented mini-narratives — big data, the sharing economy, smart cities, the Internet of Things — which are meant to fill in the intellectual and conceptual void created by the Internet narrative itself.

CAPTCHA — Completely Automated Public Turing test to tell Computers and Humans Apart.

## Nothing is less cool than data

Data analysis is the alibi of first resort for those constitutionally allergic to critical thinking.

The epistemic big-data ambition of collecting it all is both never-ending and deeply flawed. It is driven by the myth that more data automatically translates into greater truth.

Apophenia is the instinct to pick out patterns from meaningless information is essentially universal.

Our fetishization of data, which was supposed to make everything so much easier to measure, has in fact encouraged an astounding amount of chicanery.

Machine learning is a set of mathematical tools that can rival human understanding in a wide set of domains.

Machine learning, an ingenious way of disclaiming responsibility for anything. Machine learning is like money laundering for bias. It's a clean, mathematical apparatus that gives the status quo the aura of logical inevitability. The numbers don't lie.

Every line of code written comes at a price: maintenance. To avoid paying for a lot of code, we build reusable software. The problem with code re-use is that it gets in the way of changing your mind later on.

Without data, you are just another person with an opinion.

The entire statistical apparatus of the liberal media managed to get the 2016 Brexit vote and US presidential election exactly backwards.

Robert McNamara imposed on the Pentagon the same integrated system of statistical analysis he had, in the previous decade, used to rescue the Ford Motor Company.

Until after World War II, computers were literally human — a computer referred to someone (usually a woman) tasked with the tedious work of performing complex mathematical calculations.

Statisticians love to develop multiple ways of testing the same thing. If I want to decide whether two groups of people have significantly different IQs, I can run a t-test or a rank sum test or a bootstrap or a regression. You can argue about which of these is most appropriate, but I basically think that if the effect is really statistically significant and large enough to matter, it should emerge regardless of which test you use, as long as the test is reasonable and your sample isn't tiny. An effect that appears when you use a parametric test but not a non-parametric test is probably not worth writing home about. A similar lesson applies to first dates. When you're attracted to someone, you over-analyse everything you say or spend extra time trying to look attractive. But if your mutual attraction is really statistically significant and large enough to matter, it should emerge regardless of the exact circumstances of a single evening. If the shirt you wear can fundamentally alter whether someone is attracted to you, you probably shouldn't be life partners. In statistical terms, a glance at across a bar doesn't give you a lot of data and increases the probability you'll make an incorrect decision. As a statistician, I prefer not to work with small datasets, and similarly, I've never liked romantic environments that give me very little data about a person. For example, on Tinder, the only thing I can think when I see some stranger staring at me out of a phone is, "My errorbars are huge!" which makes it very hard to assess attraction. I think there's even an argument for being deliberately unattractive to your date, on the grounds that if they still like you, they must really like you.

What if somebody grabs all our statistical publications and does something with them that's not correct? Well, that's what we want! A sign of life!

## Not only are we part of nature, we're the best part

The world is not the sum of all the things in it.

The natural order is biased towards the marvellous.

Environmentalism is the indulgence of spoiled tree-huggers who lack a proper cause.

Certain environmentalist fetishes need to be exposed. Nature is not benevolent; it's indifferent. It's only through human activity, through maximising our impact, that we turn it from something for itself, into something for us — that is, we humanise it.

Impacting on the natural world, transforming and altering it, is a moral enterprise. It is part of the perpetual struggle to forge a world capable of meeting our ever-developing needs. Humanity is unnatural, if by that it is meant we are constantly freeing ourselves from natural necessity — and that's a good thing.

We are not at the edge of the end of nature, but at the end of cheap nature.

When you warn people about the dangers of climate change, they call you a saint. When you explain what needs to be done to stop it, they call you a communist.

The folk politics of climate camps, single-issue campaigns and localism have been proven to be inadequate as a response to the neoliberal conquest of state, academia and common sense.

Corporations and governments do nowadays proclaim their concern for the environment, and so do many international agencies. Conferences are held and pious resolutions passed. But to tackle ecological dangers, the depletion of resources, the overpopulation of the planet, is a task which requires very different priorities from those which move the capitalist state, not to speak of corporations. It requires an organisation of society whose dominant principle is not the drive for the maximisation of private profit; and it also requires a degree of public intervention in economic life which is anathema both to corporate and state power holders, and to international agencies inspired by neo-liberal principles.

The Casiquiare River is the only natural canal on earth to link two major river systems, the Orinoco and the Amazon.

## Symptoms are by definition unobservable

Medicine in the 20$^{th}$ century focused on healing the sick, now it is more and more focused on upgrading the healthy, which is a completely different project. It is a fundamentally different project in social and political terms, because whereas healing the sick is an egalitarian project upgrading is an elitist project. This opens the possibility of creating huge gaps between the rich and the poor. Despite this, many people say "no, it will not happen", because we have the experience of the 20$^{th}$ century, that we had many medical advances, beginning with the rich or with the most advanced countries, and gradually they trickled down to everybody, and now everybody enjoys antibiotics or vaccinations or whatever. There were peculiar reasons why medicine in the 20$^{th}$ century was egalitarian, why the discoveries trickled down to everybody. These unique conditions may not repeat themselves in the 21$^{st}$ century. When you look at the 20$^{th}$ century, it's the era of the masses, mass politics, mass economics. Every human being has value, has political, economic, and military value. This goes back to the structures of the military and of the economy, where every human being is valuable as a soldier in the trenches and as a worker in the factory. But, in the 21$^{st}$ century, there is a good chance that most humans will lose, they are losing, their military and economic value. This is true for the military, it's done, it's over. The age of the masses is over. We are no longer in the First World War, where you take millions of soldiers, give each one a rifle and have them run forward. And, the same thing perhaps is happening in the economy. Maybe the biggest question of 21$^{st}$ century economics is what will be the need in the economy for most people in the year 2050. And, once most people are no longer really necessary, for the military and for the economy, the idea that you will continue to have mass medicine is not so certain. Could be. It's not a prophecy, but you should take very seriously the option that people will lose their military and economic value, and medicine will follow.

# XI
# Tourism

## The myth of the invincibility of the white oppressor

The anti-colonial struggle in Angola ended in the mid-1970s, but was followed by 13 years of internationalised conflict — one of the most ruthless episodes of the Cold War, as decisive in its way as Vietnam or Afghanistan — involving the US, South Africa, Cuba and the Soviet Union. After an election in the early 1990s, the rebel leader Jonas Savimbi rejected the result and the country was plunged into another ten years of fighting. Peace came when Savimbi was killed in 2002.

The immediate difficulty was rivalry among the liberation movements. The MPLA — which drew support from the capital, Luanda, and a belt of country running east to the Zambian border — was at loggerheads with the Frente Naçional de Libertação de Angola (FNLA), whose base lay further north, among the Bakongo, an ethnic group on either side of Angola's border with Zaire. The MPLA was an orthodox Marxist-Leninist movement, under Soviet patronage, with an ideology that claimed to do away with racial differences: the fact remained, however, that a disproportionate number of its senior cadres were mixed race intellectuals. The FNLA clung to its Bakongo roots, which assured it a family welcome in Zaire: its leader, Holden Roberto, grew up in the Belgian Congo and married into the clan of the president, Mobutu Sese Seko. In the 1940s large numbers of Ovimbundu migrants from southern and central Angola had been brought north to work on coffee plantations, and a handful threw in their lot with the FNLA. But the ethnic strains were too great for this arrangement to last: in 1966 Jonas Savimbi, an ambitious and volatile character, left the FNLA to embark on a venture of his own, Unita (União Nacional para a Independência Total de Angola), a small Ovimbundu insurgency which later grew into the MPLA's only serious domestic adversary. Savimbi, himself a member of the Ovimbundu, would draw his support mostly from his own people to the south.

The end of Portuguese rule was hastened by a left-wing officers' coup in Lisbon in 1974. The MPLA fighting off the FNLA and Unita, in a bid to take control of Luanda and proclaim itself the first government of the new country. By now, Cold War sponsors were fully enlisted: Moscow was ready to back the MPLA, which seemed to Washington to be a Gulag brand destined to project Soviet influence across Africa. The FNLA and Unita were freedom-loving anti-Soviets. Money, arms and expertise had been flowing to Roberto's FNLA for several years, not only from Beijing and Washington, but Zaire; Unita, a marginal force at the time, quickly became a beneficiary of Washington's largesse and the fighting skills of the apartheid regime in South Africa.

In October 1975 the South African Defence Force (SADF) invaded Angola. Pretoria was determined to see off the MPLA before independence, set for the following month. Sooner or later, if the movement ended up in charge of the country, its leader, Agostinho Neto, would offer support and bases to other liberation movements in the region: not just the ANC, but the South-West Africa People's Organisation (Swapo), which had taken up arms in the name of independence for Namibia. The ANC and Swapo were firmly pro-Soviet, and Namibia — also known as South-West Africa — was a key to the titanic struggle that ensued. It had been a German colony until 1915, then a South African mandate, but when the mandate ended in the 1940s, Pretoria dug its heels in, and now ran the territory with great severity amid growing calls for independence. The South Africans were right to think that Neto would allow Swapo's guerrillas to roam freely through a newly independent Angola and right, too, that apartheid would soon be hemmed in by hostile forces unless the MPLA was crushed.

South Africa's invasion, launched from Namibia, coincided with pressure to the north from the FNLA, bolstered by more than a thousand Zairean soldiers, a contingent of gung-ho British and American mercenaries, and a detachment of South African artillery. The prospect of the two armies shaking hands in the capital over a defeated MPLA looked more than likely, and the unfolding disaster was watched with an eagle eye in Havana. Fidel Castro took a godfatherly interest in the MPLA; he'd recently posted a handful of military trainers to Angola to advise on a future national army. Now nothing short of a full-scale deployment could help Neto hold Luanda. A week before independence was due to be proclaimed Castro authorised an emergency airlift of crack units to Angola; the next few months saw a massive sea-and-air transfer of Cuban regulars and equipment. The Cubans fought Roberto and the FNLA back towards the Zaire border and pushed down to halt the South African advance. Neto and his movement were duly installed in Luanda on 11 November 1975. The FNLA were still pounding the outskirts of the city and Cuban artillery could be heard to the south as independence was declared and Portugal's last governor-general sailed away declaring that sovereignty had been transferred to the people of Angola.

Gerald Ford and Henry Kissinger, secretary of state and national security adviser at the time, had encouraged Pretoria's initiative in private, but when Cuba's arrival on the scene created a flurry of media interest there was widespread condemnation of South Africa's invasion. The US denied any collusion and joined the chorus of disapproval, while the SADF retired from Angola with few casualties and no laurels. South Africa blamed the perfidious Americans, but the real setback had been delivered by Castro's expeditionary force. By 1976 there were 36,000 Cubans in the country ready to go another round with any foreign army if necessary. Kissinger and Ford reserved their real fury for Havana. From now on no senior US figure would admit that a Cuban fighting force had deployed to defend a postcolonial government-in-waiting: for the next 13 years, as far as policy statements in Washington were concerned, Cuba was the paramount regional aggressor, working on Moscow's behalf, and the central obstacle to Namibian independence. Apartheid counted for nothing, and South Africa's illegal administration in Namibia was a secondary issue.

## APOPHTHEGM

The intervention was a bold move on Cuba's part. It was inconceivable that Castro could have behaved so provocatively, so far from home, without orders from the Soviet Union, but evidence available suggests that the opposite was the case. The Cubans had acted unilaterally, dragging Angola into a diplomatic maelstrom, upsetting the Russians, running a chill through détente, and nearly wrecking talks on strategic arms limitation. Castro adventures in Latin America had reached an impasse, while Africa still offered opportunities. Cuba had its anti-imperialist credentials to defend and its involvement on the continent was long-standing. It had sent arms to the Algerians during their anti-colonial war, and treated wounded fighters in Cuba; Che Guevara had made two quixotic forays into central Africa. Another, more successful Cuban team, led by Jorge Risquet, remained in Congo-Brazzaville for two years, much of that time training MPLA guerrillas. Pretoria's invasion, Havana's historic links with Neto's movement, and Castro's growing obsession with apartheid made Angola an inevitable destination for the Cubans.

With the South Africans gone, there was a brief respite for the new government in Luanda, but it couldn't begin to put its house in order without foreign help. The Cubans were already looking forward to the day when they could pull out, but Neto was adamant that they should stay. Having held the military line, Havana now began providing doctors, teachers and low-level managers to build the rudiments of a public administration. Angola's colonial masters had kept the population in a state of helplessness; poorer Portuguese in this settler colony had done the jobs performed by Africans in other European possessions. Eighty-five per cent of Angolans were illiterate at independence; there was almost nothing in the way of a managerial class. And the Portuguese had left en masse. In 1975 everyone who knew how to turn a screw disappeared overnight.

The only obvious asset was oil, and the MPLA were at a loss how to manage it. But in 1976, Soares de Oliveira writes, the Algerians arrived and reconfigured Angola's (efficient) colonial-statist structure into a (no less efficient) Angolan state-corporate entity, Sonangol, based on the Algerian version, Sonatrach, which was set up after the French left the country. As the US and South Africa bolstered Savimbi's rebels and the conflict began to heat up again, Sonangol remained a dependable industry regulator, handing out concessions and collecting revenues: it was insulated from doctrinaire economic policy and the envy of under-resourced ministries that wanted a share of the take, answering only to the president's office (one reason José Eduardo Dos Santos and his family became so wealthy). The president and Sonangol's management could also reassure the big Western oil companies that they had nothing to fear from a Marxist-Leninist regime — absurd as it seemed, the Cubans would end up defending French and US oil installations against sabotage efforts by the rebel factions that Paris and Washington were egging on.

Realists in Luanda recognised that a change of administration in Washington would do them no favours. With the Cubans still on the scene, Jimmy Carter was obliged to fold an ambitious hand even before he'd assumed office. As president in waiting he'd planned to push through Namibian independence, normalise relations with the MPLA and face down apartheid. In the White House, with the new national security adviser, Zbigniew Brzezinski, at his shoulder, he set all this aside. His administration was as hostile to the MPLA as Ford's had been. Shunned by the new figure in the White House but bolstered by its friends, the MPLA now made good on its offer of support to the Zimbabwe African People's Union — Rhodesia had another four years of minority rule to go — and apartheid's sworn enemies, the ANC and Swapo.

It's easy, years later, to underestimate the importance of Angola's stance on white domination. In 1975, the newly independent regimes in Mozambique and Angola were fêted in South Africa's townships. Now this disbelief vanished overnight. The 1976 Soweto uprising, a turning point in the South African struggle, was symptomatic of the mood, and after it was put down a steady trickle of South African militants made their way to Angola, where Cuban military instructors put them through their paces. Like the new government in Mozambique, the MPLA was an upstart regime which crossed a line by asserting the rights of non-white majorities in South Africa, Namibia and Rhodesia. The prospect of racial equality was suddenly real to a generation of Africans and the MPLA's regional anti-racist stance was celebrated in Africa long after it dawned on the Angolan leadership that they'd engineered a resource grab by securing the oil and the country's diamonds.

In the West, too, the anti-apartheid movement welcomed independence. Solidarity with the ANC was extended to the new democratic socialist regimes in Mozambique and Angola: their hand-me-down party structures, their Potemkin village statist economies, their hard-currency stores full of Johnnie Walker and Lithuanian pickles, and their modernisation plans for peasant agriculture were not condemned out of hand by supporters in Europe. Nor was much said about repression. The MPLA moved hard on dissenters, including enthusiastic young leftists whose ideas were thought to be too radical.

The MPLA weren't necessarily hallucinating when they saw adversaries everywhere; but notions of the enemy within were a source of anxiety, and the movement's high-mindedness was matched by its prickly sensitivities. Two splinter groups already existed before it raised the new flag in Luanda, and two top figures, Mário Pinto de Andrade and Viriato da Cruz, both accomplished poets writing in Portuguese, had fallen out with Neto, also an accomplished poet writing in Portuguese. An important guerrilla commander in the field, Daniel Chipenda, also fell out with the intransigent Neto, creating a new split in this fissile movement on the eve of Portugal's handover. After independence Neto and his loyalists were firmly in command of the movement, but mistrust and suspicion were kept alive by a bunker mentality.

South Africa had retired for the time being. Nevertheless the new government still had two dangerous adversaries in Zaire: the FNLA, which was licking its wounds, and Unita. Savimbi's movement had begun building its capacity in the south, with help from Pretoria and Washington. Congress had outlawed military aid to any non-government beneficiary in Angola, and so for the next ten years US assistance was covert: Unita, trained by South Africa's officer corps, would soon be the sole beneficiary. Confined in the capital, wondering when the next blow would fall, the MPLA turned in on itself yet again.

There was no relief from the tensions of tribe and ethnicity, which had shaped the liberation movements in Angola, as they had elsewhere.

But in Angola gradations of skin colour added a dangerous layer of difficulty. Could the MPLA, a movement with mestiço intellectuals in senior positions, represent a majority-black African nation without reproducing the condescension of the country's former colonial masters and acquiring their privileges? Mixed race citizens were closer by a degree, or three or four, to the former colonial masters. Many had enjoyed the fruits of assimilation — a good education, a route up through the system — denied to people with darker skins. Like the ANC, Neto and his entourage dealt with this large obstacle by proposing national liberation, not race liberation. Race was merely a shadow cast by the unfinished business of class struggle, and under new management the postcolonial nation-state would complete the job.

In 1977 identity politics erupted through the crust of the MPLA's Marxism-Leninism, with a failed coup by a dissident faction. It was followed by a long, under-reported bout of repression, during which the MPLA killed untold numbers of people. Neto was an absolutist who demanded total loyalty from his côterie, but debate and disputation had remained lively in the movement as a whole. Now, however, fear and reticence took hold. The MPLA — a movement known for the eloquence of its thinkers and writers — had shed the remains of its intellectual glamour, with a campaign of reprisals against real and imagined enemies at home magnified out of all proportion by the presence of menacing shadows at the edge of the picture: the rebel opposition in the bush, the intransigence of Washington, the ambivalence of Moscow, and the certainty that South Africa would strike again. The leadership emerged from this brutal interlude as an unselfconscious force, a new and ruthless creature in southern Africa. It was adapting to a hostile environment at supernatural speed and evolving as a rare specimen, able to hold its own in a world of charismatic predators. Its future at the time was unclear, but the MPLA went on to perform a crucial function in the regional ecology: to defend its habitat and bring apartheid's foreign adventures to the point of exhaustion.

A few weeks before the coup failed, Neto encouraged a group of Zairois exiled in Angola to march across the border and foment rebellion. The move put an end to any hope of improved relations with Washington: Mobutu was a staunch US ally. Carter enlisted the help of France and together they urged Morocco to send in troops. An expedition, assembled at the double by King Hassan II, drove the rebels from Zaire.

The Cubans let Neto know how rash they considered his dispatch of armed exiles to Zaire. But then in May 1978 there was a second foray by an even larger group, setting off from Angolan soil and entering Zaire via Zambia. Chivvied by Brzezinski, Carter rounded on Cuba and accused it of complicity. The Russians were exasperated too, and the Cubans were caught off-guard: how could Neto have approved an attack on Zaire without thinking through the diplomatic repercussions for his allies? Worse, he had promised it wouldn't happen again. The Ministry of Defence in Havana shot off a cable:

More than once, we have expressed our concern that the Katangans [the Zairois expatriates] could create problems for the People's Republic of Angola. We trust in your honesty, Comrade President, and therefore we do not doubt that you are true to your word. But we don't understand how entire battalions, thousands of men based in Angola, could enter Zaire without the approval of some Angolan authorities.

There was more to the flurry of recriminations than a skirmish in Zaire; Castro had recently sent troops to the new Marxist regime in Ethiopia, to combat a secession in the Ogaden, and Cuba's growing footprint in Africa was angering Washington. In the early 1960s Castro could play the anti-imperialist on the continent without alarming the US in the way that his Latin American crusade had done, but Washington now had its eye on Africa. It's not clear whether Neto weighed these questions when he went behind the backs of his patrons, as he sometimes did. The KGB did not trust him, he was not a pliant figure in the hands of their apparatchiks. The new invasion was quickly beaten back by a combined force of French and Belgians, but it achieved the effect that Neto wanted. Cowed by the second threat in less than 14 months, Mobutu agreed to a deal: the Angolans would disarm the exiles, and he would throw out the FNLA. Unita's weapons caches were dispersed and Beijing was informed that it could no longer move arms through Zaire to Savimbi — still a self-proclaimed champion of Maoism. Without Mobutu, the FNLA was finished, but Savimbi had a following — and a future — in the south of Angola: he would now get most of what he needed from the apartheid regime.

The South Africans had been happy to let the dust settle after the international stir their invasion caused, but in 1978 they struck again with a raid on a Namibian encampment at Cassinga, in southern Angola, about 150 miles north of the border. The operation began with a series of bombing and strafing runs; an airborne assault by paratroopers followed. Cubans from a nearby military base rushed to the camp and the paras fell back, but the operation was a success: at the end of the day 16 Cubans and 600 Namibians were dead. The camp was run by Swapo and undoubtedly contained fighters, but there were also large numbers of refugees: civilians had been moving north across the border as South African repression intensified in Namibia. Cassinga was a rapid-deployment massacre. It signalled that the SADF had recovered its form and the war in Angola was set to intensify.

One of the mysteries until now has been how Cuba funded its presence in Angola, from the mid-1970s until the last contingent of soldiers left in 1991. The Havana archive clears this up. It was said in the day that they were a mercenary force, which could access the diamonds, or fleece the MPLA of its oil revenue as the Angolan people starved — and they did — or alternatively that the Russians bankrolled the whole expedition. These assertions were driven mostly by anti-communist ideology.

Moscow's price for keeping the MPLA supplied with weapons between 1975 and a pre-election ceasefire in 1991 was $6 billion, most of it on credit: when the Soviet Union ceased to exist the Russians were $4 billion out of pocket. In addition Moscow kept the Cuban arsenal topped up. The Cubans were their own quartermasters in Angola, although in the early years Raúl Castro reminded Neto that they were also feeding large numbers of Angolan soldiers and feeling the pinch. Three years in, it was agreed that Cuba would pay the salaries of its own soldiers and the MPLA would take care of the rest: food, billeting and transport to and from Angola. Castro drew down the deployment in the late 1970s, and was always on the lookout for an opportunity to pull out, but as Neto admitted, the chance of a conscript army with a few Russian advisers prevailing in the event of another South African

## APOPHTHEGM

invasion was less than zero.

When Neto went to Havana in 1979, he got a presidential lecture from Fidel: "I tell you in all sincerity that you must intensify your training of Fapla (the Forças Armadas Populares de Libertação de Angola), because, look, Comrade Neto, you pay a price for our presence, and it is also a great sacrifice for us. The problem is not just economic. We have to ask tens of thousands of our men to leave the country for a year, 18 months, two years. The cost in human terms is enormous. Therefore I urge you to do everything you can to prepare Fapla, so that one day, we will be able to withdraw our troops."

But with Fapla painfully slow to get the measure of its enemies, that day was a long way off. Neto, who had begged the Cubans to stay, died in Moscow, where he was being treated for cancer. A shrewd, tyrannical figure who had estranged the Cubans more than once, and the Russians often, was replaced by an undistinguished apparatchik, trained as a petroleum engineer in Baku, and apparently better disposed to the Russians. José Eduardo dos Santos, however, filled an important requirement of the succession: like his predecessor, he was black; a mixed race president would have laid the MPLA open to even stronger accusations of racial elitism than it was subject to already.

In the meantime thousands of Cuban aid workers and technical assistants had been pouring into the country. Havana had begun by feeding them out of its own budget, bearing the cost of flights and paying their salaries at home. But the aid and technical mission in Angola — a country with 14 doctors and 6.4 million people at the time of independence — was vastly larger than any other Cuban mission, and the cost of keeping troops in the country was already $100 million a year. Under pressure, the MPLA agreed to pay the civilian salaries, anything between $250 and $1200 a month (a Cuban nurse earned $630). That was a gain for Havana: something in the order of seven thousand Cubans who would have been on the state payroll at home were now on the MPLA's, but it did nothing to offset Cuba's military expenditure.

According to the civilian aid agreement, half the Cubans' salaries were to be paid in kwanzas, the local, non-convertible currency. The official exchange rates were a joke and besides, there was very little to buy in Angola. Aid salaries paid by the MPLA were trucked to the Cuban Embassy, where great wads of kwanzas must have lined the corridors. Jorge Risquet, who ran the civilian mission in Angola, told Dos Santos: "We have a lot of kwanzas that we have received for the technical assistance, and we have nowhere to spend them. Our ambassador is a millionaire." The Cuban cooperantes had no dollars to convert on the black market. Their lifestyle in Angola was lean. Many nevertheless agreed to renew their contracts. As for the Cuban military, service in Angola was presented as a comrade's choice. But, officers who turned it down were cashiered. Rank and file who declined ran into a bureaucratic ceiling on their way up through Cuba's party structures. Angola was Castro's last and greatest internationalist adventure and it paid to go along with his vision of a post-apartheid solution on a distant continent.

With the arrival of the Reagan administration in 1981, pressure on the MPLA and Cuba redoubled. Reagan hailed Savimbi as a freedom fighter and signalled to South Africa that race segregation was a minor sin in a freedom-loving country doing its bit to defeat international communism. Pretoria set aside its worries that the US would betray it again, as it had in 1975: the SADF committed more personnel, intelligence and firepower to Savimbi and his movement, building up his base in southern Angola and accompanying his fighters on their wrecking sprees in the centre of the country, which threw Fapla into disarray, terrorised civilians and destroyed the crumbling remains of the railways, roads and electricity supply.

Castro had removed thousands of troops, but the drawdown now came to a halt. In 1982 Washington put their cards on the table: no more Cuban support for guerrillas in El Salvador and Colombia, break with the Sandinista regime in Nicaragua and clear out of Angola. The Cubans announced that they were happy to talk further. But Castro remained braced engrossed in a war in Africa. Defeat would be humiliating: apartheid victorious, its puppet regime installed in Angola, the ANC and Swapo forced to pack their bags, the Reagan doctrine of total victory over communism roundly endorsed by success in southern Africa, and independence for Namibia deferred or debased as a fig-leaf deal that left apartheid's subalterns intact. Unable to face this prospect Castro redoubled his interest in military affairs. The more personnel, intelligence and firepower South Africa threw behind Unita, the greater his insistence on clear-cut military dispositions.

The goal of the Angolan army, in the Cuban view, was to become an effective counterinsurgency force, swatting off Savimbi's offensives, giving chase and mopping up the remnants. The role of the comrade guests was to stand up to a repeat of the South African invasion in 1975. That meant deploying Cubans in southern Angola to form a line of defence north of the Namibian border. But this division of duties was liable to fray. Fapla's helplessness during the early years forced Cubans into combat against Unita, which was going from strength to strength under South African tutelage. Increasingly South African contingents were out in the field, supporting rebel infiltrations, compromising the clarity the Cubans preferred.

The Soviet Union was another Cuban headache. It had around 11,000 military advisers in Angola — all forbidden to fight — and held firmly to the belief that Fapla should become a conventional army marching this way and that, on well-planned campaigns with long supply lines, plenty of troops and armour, and the potential to go into battle anywhere. From Moscow, the Soviet chiefs of staff envisaged the kind of war in Angola that the Warsaw Pact countries might have to fight in Europe. The Soviet Union's sponsorship of Fapla meant that its opinions weighed heavily with Dos Santos and the Angolan generals, who found the idea of a large national fighting force seductive. The Cubans would tell the Angolans they will stop a South African invasion, so they should focus on the war against the Unita. The Cubans would also say that they don't need a conventional army. But the Angolans wanted a strong army, a conventional army. Over the years Soviet advice and training created a fighting force of about 80,000 to 90,000, with a respectable officer corps and a few dozen good, disciplined brigades.

As a last resort the Cubans would argue that they had historic experience as insurgents. The Cubans haven't always agreed with Russians. The Cubans poked fun at the Soviet posture in Angola, arguing that

Russian war plans were drawn up for another era and another place. The Cubans ridiculed a scheme to retake a one-horse town held by Unita as a rerun of the Red Army's operation against Berlin. The Cubans thought that the Russians underestimated the Unita and concentrated on creating a big army with many tanks, guns, and artillery. Troops who knew how to parade. Soviet campaign maps, with lots of wishful arrows scrawled in, were a running joke among the Cuban officers. If the Soviets' campaign in Afghanistan it was anything like the one in Angola, it was no wonder that victory eluded them.

Namibia was the ostensible focus of US diplomacy, but the primary objective was to force the Cubans out of Angola and ensure the collapse of the regime. Carter had thrown his weight behind UN Resolution 435, calling for independence, but the proposal had a hole under the waterline: it envisaged South Africa hanging on to part of the territory. The process was bogged down as Swapo continued its ineffectual struggle from Angola and the South Africans pursued an internal solution based on a compliant, neocolonial parliament in Namibia with friendly MPs running the show. The Reagan administration had its own plan, known as linkage, thought up by Chester Crocker, the assistant secretary of state for African affairs. He sketched it out to the South Africans shortly after he took office: no independence for Namibia until all foreign troops had left Angolan soil. In conversations with Pretoria, whose military commitment to Savimbi put hundreds of special forces in Angola, this came to mean that Resolution 435 would be stalled until the last Cubans had packed their bags. Crocker must have known that the moment they did so, South African forces would storm through Angola behind their Unita auxiliaries, and proclaim a victory for Savimbi, whereupon Namibian independence — in which Savimbi had no interest — could be postponed indefinitely. Linkage was the lynchpin of Washington's constructive engagement with apartheid, and a blessing in the eyes of Pik Botha, South Africa's foreign minister.

The policy put the MPLA and the Cubans on the spot by suggesting that the fate of Namibia no longer lay in Washington's hands, and certainly not in Pretoria's; it was up to Luanda and Havana. But, Crocker's objectives and Pretoria's never fully coincided. Washington's priority was to get the Cubans out of Angola. The South Africans hoped only to stall independence. There was nothing in Crocker's policy to nudge them from their default preference, which was to topple the MPLA and have Savimbi disband Swapo's bases. Seven years after it was mooted, Pik Botha argued that linkage — and its stress on the Cuban factor over all others — had given apartheid a shield against sanctions. By then he was defending the last ditch: the divestment and sanctions movement in America had inflicted a defeat on the Reagan administration and a bitter, telegenic struggle was underway in South Africa's townships. The only person who didn't seem to grasp its significance was Reagan.

Namibia had become a torment for the MPLA: they'd signed up as the benefactors of Swapo and the ANC with internationalist bravado, and had no doubt come to regret it, but with Reagan in office there was now a fight to the death in southern Africa, and the Cubans were on the ground to ensure there was no faint-heartedness. But Soviet military grandstanding wasn't helping the internationalist cause. In August 1983 the South Africans and Unita launched an attack on Cangamba, a small outpost in the south-east, pitting 6,000 of Savimbi's fighters, with SADF advisers and special forces, against 800 Fapla troops and 100 Cubans. After an Alamo-like resistance, Unita fell back with heavy casualties. The dust had barely settled when the row began. Castro cabled Dos Santos: "We have achieved a great victory. Now we must be practical." He called for a withdrawal from Cangamba in short order: if troops remained in place the South Africans would take to the air and avenge the defeat, in a town with no anti-aircraft defence in an isolated position 250 km from the lines. The Russians disagreed: they announced that Fapla should take advantage of the enemy's disarray and give pursuit, across a wilderness that was largely under Unita control.

Castro cabled his generals from Havana: "You must insist with the Angolans that it would be a grave error to keep a Fapla unit in Cangamba, that your orders are to withdraw the Cubans, all the Cubans, at once, even if they decide to keep a Fapla unit there. We are shocked by the words of the head of the Soviet military mission. They reflect a complete lack of realism. We cannot let more Cubans die, nor can we risk a grievous defeat because of absurd decisions.

Raúl Castro followed up with a categorical order to withdraw. In theory the final word belonged with Dos Santos, who was sitting on his hands as his two allies came to blows. Exhausted Fapla troops looked on in dismay as the Cubans pulled out. Two days later, while Fapla prepared for their march into nowhere, the South African air force pounded the town and Savimbi was able to claim a victory. It was a disaster in all but one respect: the Africa section of the Central Committee in Moscow now agreed that the Cubans had a point and so, when Jorgé Risquet went to the Soviet Union to beg for more and better weapons, he was taken seriously.

Five years of military escalation followed, during which the Reagan administration lifted the ban on arms transfers and gave Savimbi $25 million and the Stinger ground-to-air missile: if it was good enough for their friends the mujahedin in Afghanistan, it was good enough for Unita. The Cubans continued to insist that Moscow should supply Fapla with better fighter-bombers and upgrade its anti-aircraft weapons, in order to equal or perhaps exceed South African air power.

A few months into 1988, in the airstrip in Menongue MiG-23s took off on a sortie over South African positions. The woodland quivered to a thunderstorm that seemed to erupt from the ground; as the planes gained altitude there was a long concussion in the sky. These terrifying engines of harm taking to the wing produced a strong, partisan sensation. Castro had got what he'd asked for from Moscow.

Everyone was talking about the battle of Cuito Cuanavale, a miserable settlement an hour or so to the south of Menongue. The settlement, with its crucial forward airstrip, came under siege from Unita battalions, long-range South African artillery and aerial bombardment. Unita forces went around the back of the town and cut the road to Menongue. If Cuito Cuanavale fell, the south-east of Angola would fall with it and in due course half the country would be lost to Unita and South Africa. Mandela came to define this battle as the turning point for the liberation of the African continent from the scourge of apartheid.

## APOPHTHEGM

The South Africans were heavily committed: besides their special forces, there were several mechanised infantry units, scores of regular conscripts and a contingent of Namibian territorials, reassigned from repressive duties at home: about 5,000 men in all. The guns thundered, there were thousands of casualties and there was everything to play for.

The South Africans came close to capturing the settlement, but crucially they lost the tempo. When Fapla was turned back from the Lomba River with such ease, the SADF's original notion — to hold up the enemy offensive — gave way to something more ambitious. Chris Thirion of South African Military Intelligence explained that the South African plans changed when everything went so well. It was decided, halfway through the battle to take Cuito. In September P.W. Botha was flown up to southern Angola to congratulate his men and he gave the go-ahead for the total destruction of the enemy forces north of the Lomba and the advance to and possible capture of Cuito Cuanavale itself.

The scale of this new objective called for more resources. The SADF took note and refrained from immediate pursuit of the retreating Fapla brigades: better, certainly, to comply with the president's big vision, hang fire and wait for reinforcements, which would allow it to finish the job with a flourish and carve a flank out of Angolan territory, where Savimbi could announce partition and a rival state. But delay had a fatal, unforeseen flaw: it allowed the remains of capable Fapla battalions to withdraw to Cuito Cuanavale and reassemble. Within days, 1500 Cubans had joined them to reorganise the defences, as other Fapla units arrived from the north. In the time it took for the South Africans to bring up their own reinforcements, the airstrip at Cuito Cuanavale had been repaired and the town resupplied.

The Cubans were no longer consulting Moscow, there were informing them. Had the Russians failed to supply it there would have been a decisive rift between Moscow and a valuable, if difficult ally; the Cubans would have been at the mercy of enemy air power and heavy losses could have been expected. The internationalist blood and treasure already poured into Angola outweighed any argument for going back;

the Russians sighed and fell in behind their unpredictable comrades. With the siege underway the Cubans planned a risky initiative of their own: not in the south-east, where the fighting was furious and the grandiose, Soviet-inspired campaigns had failed, but miles off to the west, well below the Cuban line, where he could circumvent Unita by running experienced soldiers and good weaponry along the Namibian border and come face to face with his enemy of choice: South Africa.

By the beginning of 1988, as the SADF moved up its reinforcements and the siege intensified, the Cubans were remaking the architecture of the war above the skyline: their pilots were flying the new MiGs. According to the SADF and others, their strikes were unimpressive, but their presence — and the sophisticated mobile anti-aircraft systems now at Cuba's disposal — forced the South African air force to play a very cautious game. On the ground, in March, SADF armour ran into a minefield as it advanced on Cuito Cuanavale. Three or four tanks were lost, and the South Africans withdrew in disarray. Abandoning expensive armour short of the objective was a symbolic blow for a military culture founded on white supremacist values and thrifty housekeeping, no matter how many Fapla the SADF had killed, how much Soviet matériel lay strewn in the bush, or how many black South African protesters were being detained at home.

News of the setback spread quickly through the region, where it was spun as a rout. In South Africa it was greeted with the kind of exuberance R.W. Johnson describes at the time of independence in Mozambique and Angola, two million lives and 13 years earlier. The canny, unbeatable white man and Savimbi, his unscrupulous bearer, were on the back foot and the comrades in South Africa's townships rejoiced. Castro too was gloating: South Africa had been banging on the doors of Cuito Cuanavale for four months.

The bridge across the little river was destroyed by South African artillery. Makeshift pontoons were put up, shelled and replaced, but the Cubans and Angolans maintained a presence on the forward bank. The defences held, the road to Menongue was secured, and South Africa's offensive ground to an inauspicious halt. As Pretoria prepared to rewrite the history of a missed opportunity, Castro put his cherished plan into action and began deploying his new draft of Cubans, plus anti-aircraft systems, close to the Namibian border. The balance of power in the air had changed and the Cuban threat on the ground was worrying enough for the press in South Africa to ask whether their boys in Angola could get home without a costly confrontation.

Negotiations between the US, South Africa, Angola and Cuba were already underway in 1988, but it took a clash on the Namibian border to bring the talks to fruition. In June, SADF tanks attacked a Cuban patrol hard on the frontier and South African artillery bombarded along the new Cuban front. The Cubans retaliated with an air strike against South African positions in Angola. Apartheid forces, anticipating an incursion into Namibia, blew up a bridge on the Cunene River.

Four weeks later, at a meeting of defence officials from Washington, Luanda, Havana and Pretoria in Cape Verde, South Africa was offered a choice: they could have it out with the Cubans on the battlefield or acquiesce to the enemy's terms — no ceasefire until the SADF left Angola. Geldenhuys consulted with Pretoria and folded the following day. South Africa agreed to pull out all its forces by September.

South Africa's withdrawal revived the stalled negotiations. In 1989 Namibian elections gave Swapo a resounding victory and in 1990 Mandela was released. Events moved so rapidly that it's easy to elide the connection between apartheid's military failure in Angola and its political retreat at home 14 months later. Yet the successful defence of Cuito Cuanavale had bought Castro his ticket to push down towards Namibia and put immense pressure on apartheid's negotiators. The outcome of a long ideological contest that rallied the West behind apartheid against an inexperienced, ruthless group of postcolonial activists, backed by Cuba with the Soviet Union in tow, was determined on the ground.

The pending collapse of the Soviet Union played its part in the regional settlement, but Moscow was still pouring in arms when the Cubans took matters into their own hands, and Mandela never failed to thank them for their role. The outcome in Angola destroyed the myth of the invincibility of the white oppressor.

## The European colonial powers of the 1880s became the colonies of the United States by 1945

The nation functions as an imaginary community that compensates for the lack of real liberty or equality of its members.

The nation is an imagined political community and imagined as both inherently limited and sovereign. It is imagined because the members of even the smallest nation will never know their fellow-members, meet them, or even hear of them, yet in the minds of each lives the image of their communion. The nation is imagined as a community, because, regardless of the actual inequality and exploitation that may prevail in each, the nation is conceived as a deep, horizontal comradeship. It is this fraternity that makes it possible, over the past two centuries for so many millions of people, not so much to kill, as willing to die for such limited imaginings.

Left to itself, the logic of the capitalist struggle between firms (and its inherent tendency to escalate to the level of states) can only be internecine war. Once can come to the conclusion that the future of the system must — in its own interests — lie in the emergence of mechanisms of international capitalist coordination capable of transcending such conflicts — ultra-imperialism. This was a prospect that can be easily rejected as utopian. The second half of the 20$^{th}$ century it became clear that the coordination problem can be satisfactorily resolved only by the existence of a superordinate power, capable of imposing discipline on the system as a whole, in the common interests of all parties. Such imposition cannot be a product of brute force. It must also correspond to a genuine capacity of persuasion — ideally, a form of leadership that can offer the most advanced model of production and culture of its day, as target of imitation for all others. That is the definition of hegemony, as a general unification of the field of capital.

The UN logo, showing a map of the globe within a wreath of flowers, was carefully designed to exclude Argentina from view because of its friendship with Nazi Germany.

Ambassadors are persons who having failed to secure an office from the people are given one by the Administration on condition that they leave the country.

The division of the world into rich and poor regions roughly follows the former boundaries between imperial and colonised areas, even though it has sometimes been partially counteracted or qualified by resistance or by prior institutional or natural endowments. The colonial experience weakened the ability of the colonised to negotiate an advantageous relationship to the emergence of a capitalist world market, and often condemned them to subordination and neglect.

The fall of Communism in the East thus witnessed the extinction of the last literate societies in Europe.

Inscriptions and bird droppings are the only two things in Egypt that give any indication of life.

The protests to celebrate the military coup in Egypt were the largest mass protests in human history.

Israel is democratic towards Jews, and Jewish towards Arabs.

North Korea is a hipsters' paradise: everyone has single-gear bikes and vintage clothes. There are plenty of solar panels and almost no cars. North Korea is the future!

Deng Xiaoping had a strategy to use capitalism to build a radically different society: infrared rather than red.

Mao Tse-tung is the Wade-Giles spelling, and Mao Zedong is the pinyin spelling. China officially adopted pinyin for transliterating Chinese around 1978. Before that date, Wade-Giles was more widely used.

## Impoverished European countries expect the developed West European ones to bear the full burden of multicultural openness, while they can afford patriotism

The European Union fails to satisfy any of the democratic requirements it imposes on its member states.

In a democracy, the people must be able to determine government and legislation in free and equal elections. This core content may be complemented by plebiscitary voting on factual issues. In a democracy, the decision of the people is the focal point of the formation and retention of political power: every democratic government knows the fear of losing power by being voted out of office. Nothing like this exists in the EU: there are no elections or other votes that would allow the emergence of a well-organized opposition with the opportunity of coming into power with a programme of action.

Europe's soft-footed Machiavellianism: they decide on something, leave it lying around and wait and see what happens. If no one kicks up a fuss, because most people don't understand what has been decided, they continue step by step until there is no turning back.

The European Union's institutions had peace and stability as their objective now they just demand peoples be politically neutralised.

The idea that after the European Union structural reforms the Southern countries will be able to grow their economies faster than the Northern countries, without any assistance at all, is something only economists could imagine.

The European Union is the culmination of the political evolution, at all levels of authority, toward the development of a regulatory state. In this generic process, the imperatives of economic efficiency under conditions of capitalist competition compel political actors to delegate power to agencies composed of experts, independent of political parties or legislative interference. This development began in the United States toward the end of the 19$^{th}$ century and has taken some time to arrive in Western Europe, where policies of income redistribution and nationalisation were more strongly entrenched. Even the early EEC had some of these forms of policy distortion (vide the Common Agricultural Policy), but by the 1980s and the Single European Act, the EU came to recognise its fate as a regulatory polity. Indeed, the EU is an exaggerated version of this political form since it cannot be tempted by independent taxing power or coercive military capacity to adopt the alternative strategies of redistribution or nationalization. All that the Eurocrats in Brussels can aspire to is extending their regulatory grasp into new areas — producing, in the process, an acquis of some

# APOPHTHEGM

90,000 pages of directives.

The European Union has exceeded its functional mandate and got involved in matters that should be none of its business. Monetary unification may have been disguised as purely a matter of efficiency and deliberation among experts, but it was bound to generate far greater and more uneven consequences than the sort of regulation that has benefited everyone.

The European Union is following the Constitution of the People's Republic of China: the communist market economy. This system, of which China is an unsurpassable model, combines limitless economic freedom for the ruling class with a dramatic curtailment of democracy and working class rights. Europe has also adopted a Western version of what Article 1 of the Chinese Constitution calls a democratic dictatorship. The difference — obviously very important — is that this dictatorship is exercised by a single party in China and in Europe by financial markets. But this distinction does not necessarily eliminate the commonalities — including, notably, a marked aversion to trade union freedoms and the right to strike, which are the pillars of social democracy, no less likely than political democracy to disrupt the spontaneous order of the market. In the case law of the European Court, as under Communist rule, loud proclamation of the fundamental rights of workers is accompanied by prohibition of their attempts to defend their interests freely and collectively.

Modern monetary systems and practices are embedded in nation states and can differ fundamentally from one country to the next. In the case of the single currency, it will suffice to distinguish between the Mediterranean countries and those of Northern Europe, Germany in particular. The European South produced a type of capitalism in which growth was driven above all by domestic demand, supported where need be by inflation; demand was driven in turn by budget deficits, or by trade unions strengthened by high levels of job security and a large public sector. Moreover, inflation made it easier for governments to borrow, as it steadily devalued the public debt. The system was supported by a heavily regulated banking sector, partly or wholly state owned. All these things taken together made it possible to harmonise more or less satisfactorily the interests of workers and employers, who typically operated in the domestic market and on a small scale. The price for the social peace generated in this way was a loss of international competitiveness, in contrast to hard-currency countries; but with national currencies, that loss could be made good by periodic devaluations, at the expense of foreign imports. The northern economies functioned differently. Their growth came from exports, so they were inflation-averse. This applied to workers and their unions, too, despite the occasional use of Keynesian rhetoric—and all the more so in the era of globalization, when cost increases could so easily lead to production being relocated to cheaper zones. These countries do not necessarily need the option of devaluation. Despite the repeated revaluations of its currency, due in part to the revaluation of its products, the German economy has thrived since the 1970s, not least by migrating from markets that compete on price to those that compete on quality. Unlike the Mediterranean states, the hard-currency countries are wary of both inflation and debt, even though their interest rates are relatively low. Their ability to survive without a loose monetary policy benefits their numerous savers, whose votes carry significant political weight; it also means they don't need to take on the risk of market bubbles.

The European Union has acted as an uncompromising vehicle of neoliberalism. Economically it has forced an imposition of austerity on Greece and several other member states, and institutionally it has been hollowing out democratic governance.

The Greek political class has not only willingly signed up to the euro project, but that even the radical left Syriza variant of that political class treats the eurozone as Eagles' Hotel California — you can check out any time you like, but you can never leave.

Syriza went into government with a gun pointed to its own head, declaring it was prepared to pull the trigger if its demands were not met. The response of Merkel and the rest of the EU was just what would should have expected: "Okay. But not in here — we're eating. Please step outside the room and shoot yourself in the head."

The European school: in this school building children from Germany,

Belgium, France, Italy, Luxembourg and the Netherlands, and from other countries which are interested in the construction of a unified Europe, will assemble from their early childhood to the time of their university. Educated side by side, untroubled from infancy by divisive prejudices, acquainted with all that is great and good in the different cultures, it will be borne in on them as they mature that they belong together. Without ceasing to look to their own lands with love and pride, they will become in mind Europeans, schooled and ready to complete and consolidate the work of their fathers before them, to bring into being a united and thriving Europe.

## The Italians provide visitors that of feeling morally superiority

Europe, as it has become more integrated, has also become more difficult to write about.

In France writing is still first and foremost a performance of culture.

In France, drunkenness is a consequence, never an intention.

In the 19th century the Germans painted their dream and the outcome was invariably vegetable. The French needed only to paint a vegetable and it was already a dream.

Fascism represented for Italy and Germany their belated and terribly distorted version of the French Revolution.

German thinking has become indistinguishable from Western thought in general and such assimilation is one of the great political success stories of the twentieth century. The temptations and delusions of Germany as Kulturnation were eventually set aside for a sturdy adjustment to the everyday world of contemporary politics in Bonn.

The Spanish language exists only in order for Don Quixote of La Mancha to exist.

Greece might be located in Europe, but its social structure is more characteristic of a Latin American country. There is a huge urban/rural divide: the rich are more insulated from the rest of society than elsewhere in Europe, while politics is deeply embedded in informal systems of patronage and corruption.

The Irish, unlike their erstwhile colonial proprietors, have always been a cosmopolitan nation, from the nomadic monks of the Middle Ages to the corporate executives of the Celtic Tiger. If the oppressiveness of colonial rule turned some of them into nationalists, it turned others into citizens of the world.

Post-war Austria's great achievement has been to convince the world that Hitler was a German and Beethoven an Austrian.

Before the Second World War, the mini-states, like Andorra and Luxembourg and all the rest, weren't even reckoned as part of the international system, except by stamp collectors.

There is a profound sense of being left behind, neglected, unsuccessful, of being abandoned losers by East European nations. Their solution appears to be an uncritical acceptance of a fictitious, idealised West and a humble acceptance of its lead.

The Union of Soviet Socialist Republics the is first and only state in history to include no national or territorial reference in its name.

In 1956, the Russians were already halfway towards fascism.

A Bonaparte will emerge in Russia who will conquer the whole of Europe, and in 500 years everything will be just fine. That's Marcuse's way of thinking.

The two major forms of historical progress registered within world capitalism in the past fifty years — the defeat of fascism and the end of colonialism — have been directly dependent on the presence and performance of the USSR in international politics. In this sense, it could be argued that, paradoxically, the exploited classes outside the Soviet Union may have benefited more directly from its existence than the working class inside the Soviet Union: that on a world historical scale the decisive costs of Stalinism have been internal, the gains external.

## APOPHTHEGM

## The American presidency cannot be anything but imperial

The political liberties in the United States of America are largely negated by economic pressures.

The United States pushed the following agenda post 1945: first, to penetrate existing capitalist states and reorganise their internal arrangements to suit US purposes; and second, to defeat any social forces there that rejected the American path to modernity in the name, not of traditionalism, but of an alternative modernity.

The two most distinctive features of the American empire are its non-territorial character, its non-possession of a formal colonial empire; and, its possession of a formally anti-imperialist ideology sustained by an ideology of freedom. This has led to the invisibility of American imperialism when compared with the territorial colonialism of European countries.

The more clear-eyed the United States is about its interests the less savagery it is perpetrated in the name of idealism.

The United States is an empire now, and when they act, they create their own reality. And while we are studying that reality they will act again, creating other new realities, which we can study too, and that's how things will sort out. They are history's actors, and we, all of us, will be left to just study what they do.

In the international sphere, Americans have had to act as judge, jury, police, and in the case of military action, executioner. It has been since 1945, so it must be forever.

United States has no need of legal justification for its wars, for its record in defending democracy in the three decisive battles of the twentieth century — the First World War, the Second World War and the Cold War — gives its *de facto* pre-eminence an ethical legitimacy.

By the early 1970s, global capital wasn't serving the United States as effectively as the United States was serving it.

The amassing of financial reserves in Asia does not in itself signal a shift in the locus of global power; gathering resources is quite a different matter to having the structural power to shape how those resources are used.

The USSR will not be the only superpower to collapse under pressure from unchecked military spending, an unwinnable war against Saudi-rooted Islamic extremists, and an absence of legitimacy bred by rampant corruption among its elite.

American professionalism has been corrupted by the managerial capitalism with which it is so closely allied, just as professionalism in the Soviet Union has been much more completely corrupted by the dictatorship of the party.

The United States are in a state of idolisation of an ephemeral self, they are relying upon their past greatness, but this keep getting them into worse and worse social and cultural disasters.

One of the central myths of American nationalism has long been exceptionalism — the idea that the United States history, culture and political life are by definition incomparable.

The United States civil war saw the largest, uncompensated expropriation of property in American history: the abolition of slavery. Nullifying slave owners' property in persons meant returning personhood to the slaves. It also extinguished roughly half the value of all Southern assets, which in today's prices amounts to roughly $3 trillion.

The South exists so the United States as a whole can deny all its injustices by projecting to a other within the country.

The necessity of the incarnation of reason in just one world-historical state (the United States) can never entirely erase the contingent multiplicity of political forms around it.

## The historical defeat and humiliation of the British working classes is now the UK's primary export product

The lessons Britain learned in sustaining their slave-owning society were later applied in industrial England.

The British never had the capacity to reshape coercively the internal arrangements of other capitalist states. Their speciality was taking over and reshaping pre-capitalist societies, defeating traditionalist forces of resistance within them. So the principle of absolute states' rights and non-interference was perfectly acceptable to the British, once they had reached the limits of their empire.

The English people think they are free. They are deceiving themselves; they are free only during the election of members of Parliament. As soon as they are elected, the people are enslaved and count for nothing.

Those who dream of an English finger on the nuclear trigger inhabit a fantasy world: the finger will always be American.

The UK's economic growth, millions of jobs, and the welfare state itself, are dependent on the success of finance as the key mechanism by which global value is captured. Add to this real estate, and it is tempting to conclude that the UK economy is little more than a machine for the capture of value. All that Britain has bothered to produce over the last 30 years has been the arms needed to defend that machine.

Kilt is a costume sometimes worn by Scotchmen in America and Americans in Scotland.

## Hitler was a child of the first globalisation

Neoliberalism is bad when practiced in our own countries, but when imposed on other countries, it's globalisation.

The discourse of globalisation has been adopted by policymakers as a way of blaming the effects and the consequences of their own policies — aimed primarily at making the whole globe a safe playground for capital — on historical inevitability.

In its 29 year existence, around 140 people died attempting to cross the Berlin Wall. In the promised world of global economic freedom and prosperity, 412 people died crossing the U.S.-Mexican border last year alone, and more than three thousand died the previous year in the Mediterranean. Pop songs and Hollywood movies about freedom are nowhere to be found.

At the end of the twentieth century, migration had become really quite different from that in earlier periods, largely because, by emigrating, one no longer breaks links with the past to the same extent as before. You can continue living in two, possibly even three, worlds at the same time, and identify with two or three different places. You can go on being a Guatemalan while you're in the United States.

Mass tourism is the most enduring legacy of the post-war economic boom.

Travelling is the key for the building of an individual, but to travel without understanding is only key to the tourism industry.

The tourist arrives to observe monuments to glory, not interrogate the very notion of glory.

There is strong experimental evidence in favour of the conjecture from the fact that we have not been invaded by hordes of tourists from the future.

# XII
# Past

## The killing of Osama bin Laden

The killing of Osama bin Laden was the high point of Obama's first term, and a major factor in his re-election. The White House saw the mission as an all-American affair, where senior generals of Pakistan's army and Inter-Services Intelligence agency (ISI) were not told of the raid in advance. This is false, as are many other elements of the Obama administration's account.

Here is the true story: bin Laden had been a prisoner of the ISI at the Abbottabad compound since 2006; Pakistan's two most senior military leaders — General Ashfaq Parvez Kayani, chief of the army staff, and General Ahmed Shuja Pasha, director general of the ISI — knew of the raid in advance and had made sure that the two helicopters delivering the Seals to Abbottabad could cross Pakistani airspace without triggering any alarms; the CIA did not learn of bin Laden's whereabouts by tracking his couriers, as the White House has claimed since May 2011, but from a former senior Pakistani intelligence officer who betrayed the secret in return for much of the $25 million reward offered by the US; and, while Obama did order the raid and the Seal team did carry it out, many other aspects of the administration's account were false.

It all began with a walk-in. In August 2010 a former senior Pakistani intelligence officer approached Jonathan Bank, then the CIA's station chief at the US embassy in Islamabad. He offered to tell the CIA where to find bin Laden in return for the reward that Washington had offered in 2001. Walk-ins are assumed by the CIA to be unreliable, and the response from the agency's headquarters was to fly in a polygraph team. The walk-in passed the test.

The US initially kept what it knew from the Pakistanis. The fear was that if the existence of the source was made known, the Pakistanis themselves would move bin Laden to another location. So only a very small number of people were read into the source and his story. The CIA's first goal was to check out the quality of the informant's information. The compound was put under satellite surveillance. The CIA rented a house in Abbottabad to use as a forward observation base and staffed it with Pakistani employees and foreign nationals.

In October 2010, Obama was briefed on the intelligence. His response was cautious. For Obama it just made no sense that bin Laden was living in Abbottabad. It was just too crazy. The president instructed the CIA to have proof that it was really bin Laden. This became the immediate goal of the CIA leadership and the Joint Special Operations Command so they could get Obama's support. They believed they would get this if they got DNA evidence, and if they could assure Obama that a night assault of the compound would carry no risk. However, the only way to accomplish both things — DNA and a night assault — was to get the Pakistanis on board.

During the late autumn of 2010, the US continued to keep quiet about the walk-in, and Kayani and Pasha continued to insist to their American counterparts that they had no information about bin Laden's whereabouts. The next step was to figure out how to ease Kayani and Pasha into it — to tell them that the US had the intelligence showing that there is a high-value target in the compound, and to ask them what they know about the target. It didn't take long to get the co-operation, because the Pakistanis wanted to ensure the continued release of American military aid, a good percentage of which was anti-terrorism funding that finances personal security, such as bullet-proof limousines and security guards and housing for the ISI leadership. There were also under-the-table personal incentives that were financed by off-the-books Pentagon contingency funds.

The US turned for help to Kayani and Pasha, who asked Amir Aziz — a doctor and a major in the Pakistani army — to obtain the specimens of bin Laden's DNA to form as a proof. Soon after the raid the press found out that Aziz had been living in a house near the bin Laden compound: local reporters discovered his name in Urdu on a plate on the door. Pakistani officials denied that Aziz had any connection to bin Laden, but Aziz has been rewarded with a share of the $25 million reward the US had put up because the DNA sample had showed conclusively that it was bin Laden in Abbottabad.

Bargaining continued over the way the mission would be executed. Kayani told the US that they couldn't have a big strike force. The US would have to come in lean and mean and kill bin Laden or there wouldn't have been a deal. The agreement was struck by the end of January 2011, and Joint Special Operations Command prepared a list of questions to be answered by the Pakistanis: 'How can we be assured of no outside intervention? What are the defences inside the compound and its exact dimensions? Where are bin Laden's rooms and exactly how big are they? How many steps in the stairway? Where are the doors to his rooms, and are they reinforced with steel? How thick?' The Pakistanis agreed to permit a four-man American cell — a Navy Seal, a CIA case officer and two communications specialists — to set up a liaison office at Tarbela Ghazi for the coming assault. By then, the military had constructed a mock-up of the compound in Abbottabad at a secret former nuclear test site in Nevada, and an elite Seal team had begun rehearsing for the attack.

Pasha and Kayani were responsible for ensuring that Pakistan's army and air defence command would not track or engage with the US helicopters used on the mission. The American cell at Tarbela Ghazi was charged with co-ordinating communications between the ISI, the senior US officers at their command post in Afghanistan, and the two Black Hawk helicopters; the goal was to ensure that no stray Pakistani fighter plane on border patrol spotted the intruders and took action to stop them. The initial plan said that news of the raid shouldn't be announced straightaway. All units in the Joint Special Operations

## APOPHTHEGM

Command operate under stringent secrecy and the JSOC leadership believed, as did Kayani and Pasha, that the killing of bin Laden would not be made public for as long as seven days, maybe longer. Then a carefully constructed cover story would be issued: Obama would announce that DNA analysis confirmed that bin Laden had been killed in a drone raid in the Hindu Kush, on Afghanistan's side of the border. The Americans who planned the mission assured Kayani and Pasha that their co-operation would never be made public. It was understood by all that if the Pakistani role became known, there would be violent protests — bin Laden was considered a hero by many Pakistanis — and Pasha and Kayani and their families would be in danger, and the Pakistani army publicly disgraced.

At the Abbottabad compound ISI guards were posted around the clock to keep watch over bin Laden and his wives and children. They were under orders to leave as soon as they heard the rotors of the US helicopters. The town was dark: the electricity supply had been cut off on the orders of the ISI hours before the raid began. One of the Black Hawks crashed inside the walls of the compound, injuring many on board. The Seals knew the time on target had to be tight because they would wake up the whole town going in. The cockpit of the crashed Black Hawk, with its communication and navigational gear, had to be destroyed by concussion grenades, and this would create a series of explosions and a fire visible for miles. Two Chinook helicopters had flown from Afghanistan to a nearby Pakistani intelligence base to provide logistical support, and one of them was immediately dispatched to Abbottabad. But because the helicopter had been equipped with a bladder loaded with extra fuel for the two Black Hawks, it first had to be reconfigured as a troop carrier. The crash of the Black Hawk and the need to fly in a replacement were nerve-wracking and time-consuming setbacks, but the Seals continued with their mission. There was no firefight as they moved into the compound; the ISI guards had gone. Had there been any opposition, the team would have been highly vulnerable. An ISI liaison officer flying with the Seals guided them into the darkened house and up a staircase to bin Laden's quarters. The Seals had been warned by the Pakistanis that heavy steel doors blocked the stairwell on the first and second-floor landings; bin Laden's rooms were on the third floor. The Seal squad used explosives to blow the doors open, without injuring anyone. One of bin Laden's wives was screaming hysterically and a bullet — perhaps a stray round — struck her knee. Aside from those that hit bin Laden, no other shots were fired. Osama was cowering and retreated into the bedroom. Two shooters followed him and opened up. Very simple, very straightforward, very professional hit.

After they killed bin Laden, the Seals were just there, some with physical injuries from the crash, waiting for the relief chopper. Twenty tense minutes. The Black Hawk is still burning. There are no city lights. No electricity. No police. No fire trucks. They have no prisoners. Bin Laden's wives and children were left for the ISI to interrogate and relocate. Despite all the talk, there were no garbage bags full of computers and storage devices. The Seals just stuffed some books and papers they found in his room in their backpacks. The Seals weren't there because they thought bin Laden was running a command centre for al-Qaida operations, as the White House would later tell the media. And they were not intelligence experts gathering information inside that house.

The key question became whether Obama should stand by the agreement with Kayani and Pasha and pretend a week or so later that bin Laden had been killed in a drone attack in the mountains. Or should he go public immediately. The downed helicopter made it easy for Obama's political advisers to urge the latter plan. The explosion and fireball would be impossible to hide, and word of what had happened was bound to leak. Obama had to get out in front of the story before someone in the Pentagon did: waiting would diminish the political impact.

Obama's speech was put together in a rush and was viewed by his advisers as a political document, not a message that needed to be submitted for clearance to the national security bureaucracy. This series of self-serving and inaccurate statements would create chaos in the weeks following. Obama said that his administration had discovered that bin Laden was in Pakistan through a possible lead the previous August; to many in the CIA the statement suggested a specific event, such as a walk-in. The remark led to a new cover story claiming that the CIA's brilliant analysts had unmasked a courier network handling bin Laden's continuing flow of operational orders to al-Qaida. Obama also praised a small team of Americans for their care in avoiding civilian deaths and said: "After a firefight, they killed Osama bin Laden and took custody of his body". Two more details now had to be supplied for the cover story: a description of the firefight that never happened, and a story about what happened to the corpse. Obama went on to praise the Pakistanis: "It's important to note that our counterterrorism co-operation with Pakistan helped lead us to bin Laden and the compound where he was hiding." That statement risked exposing Kayani and Pasha. The White House's solution was to ignore what Obama had said and order anyone talking to the press to insist that the Pakistanis had played no role in killing bin Laden. Obama left the clear impression that he and his advisers hadn't known for sure that bin Laden was in Abbottabad, but only had information about the possibility. This led first to the story that the Seals had determined they'd killed the right man by having a six-foot-tall Seal lie next to the corpse for comparison (bin Laden was known to be six foot four); and then to the claim that a DNA test had been performed on the corpse and demonstrated conclusively that the Seals had killed bin Laden. But, according to the retired official, it wasn't clear from the Seals' early reports whether all of bin Laden's body, or any of it, made it back to Afghanistan.

The White House press corps was told in a briefing shortly after Obama's announcement that the death of bin Laden was the culmination of years of careful and highly advanced intelligence work that focused on tracking a group of couriers, including one who was known to be close to bin Laden. Reporters were told that a team of specially assembled CIA and National Security Agency analysts had traced the courier to a highly secure million-dollar compound in Abbottabad. After months of observation, the American intelligence community had high confidence that a high-value target was living in the compound, and it was assessed that there was a strong probability that it was Osama bin Laden. The US assault team ran into a firefight on entering the compound and three adult males — two of them believed to be the couriers — were slain, along with bin Laden. Asked if bin Laden had defended himself, one of the briefers said yes: "He did resist the assault force. And he was killed in a firefight."

The next day John Brennan, then Obama's senior adviser for counterterrorism, had the task of talking up Obama's valour while trying to smooth over the misstatements in his speech. He provided a more detailed but equally misleading account of the raid and its planning. Speaking on the record, which he rarely does, Brennan said that the mission was carried out by a group of Navy Seals who had been instructed to take bin Laden alive, if possible. He said the US had no information suggesting that anyone in the Pakistani government or military knew bin Laden's whereabouts: "We didn't contact the Pakistanis until after all of our people, all of our aircraft were out of Pakistani airspace." He emphasised the courage of Obama's decision to order the strike, and said that the White House had no information that confirmed that bin Laden was at the compound before the raid began. Obama, he said, made what I believe was one of the gutsiest calls of any president in recent memory. Brennan increased the number killed by the Seals inside the compound to five: bin Laden, a courier, his brother, a bin Laden son, and one of the women said to be shielding bin Laden.

None of the Seals thought that Obama was going to get on national TV and announce the raid. The Special Forces command was apoplectic. They prided themselves on keeping operational security. There was fear in Special Operations that if the true story of the missions leaked out, the White House bureaucracy was going to blame it on the Seals. The White House's solution was to silence the Seals. On 5 May, every member of the Seal hit team — they had returned to their base in southern Virginia — and some members of the Joint Special Operations Command leadership were presented with a nondisclosure form drafted by the White House's legal office; it promised civil penalties and a lawsuit for anyone who discussed the mission, in public or private. Admiral William McRaven, who was then in charge of JSOC, was apoplectic. He knew he was fucked by the White House, but he's a dyed-in-the-wool Seal, and not then a political operator, and he knew there's no glory in blowing the whistle on the president. When Obama went public with bin Laden's death, everyone had to scramble around for a new story that made sense, and the planners were stuck holding the bag.

Within days, some of the early exaggerations and distortions had become obvious and the Pentagon issued a series of clarifying statements. No, bin Laden was not armed when he was shot and killed. And no, bin Laden did not use one of his wives as a shield. The press by and large accepted the explanation that the errors were the inevitable by-product of the White House's desire to accommodate reporters frantic for details of the mission.

One lie that has endured is that the Seals had to fight their way to their target. To complete the cover up, The Pentagon report, which was put online in June 2013, noted that Admiral McRaven had ordered the files on the raid to be deleted from all military computers and moved to the CIA, where they would be shielded from FOIA requests by the agency's operational exemption.

The killing of bin Laden was political theatre designed to burnish Obama's military credentials. We should have expected the political grandstanding. It's irresistible to a politician. If Obama had gone ahead with the cover story, there would have been no need to have a funeral within hours of the killing. Once the cover story was blown, and the death was made public, the White House had a serious "Where's the body?" problem. The world knew US forces had killed bin Laden in Abbottabad. Panic city. What to do? They needed a functional body because they needed to reassure the public that they identified bin Laden via a DNA analysis. It was navy officers that came up with the burial at sea idea. Perfect. No body and a honourable burial following sharia law. Burial is made public in great detail, but Freedom of Information documents confirming the burial are denied for reasons of national security. It's the classic unravelling of a poorly constructed cover story — it solves an immediate problem but, given the slightest inspection, there is no back-up support. There never was a plan, initially, to take the body to sea, and no burial of bin Laden at sea took place. If the Seals' first accounts are to be believed, there wouldn't have been much left of bin Laden to put into the sea in any case.

It was inevitable that the Obama administration's lies, misstatements and betrayals would create a backlash. The US suffered a four-year lapse in co-operation with Pakistan. It has taken long for the Pakistanis to trust the US again in the military-to-military counterterrorism relationship. Pakistan felt that Obama sold them down the river.

## We learn from history that we do not learn from history

History is the ordeal to which mankind is subjected while awaiting the apocalypse.

Reality is just a story people tell themselves.

The mind of a man will desperately struggle to create memories where none exist.

We are focused with the immense difficulty, if not the impossibility, of verifying the past. Not just merely years ago, but yesterday, this morning.

It is impossible to understand the world today until today has become tomorrow.

World history can be divided into three epochs: pre-horse, horse, and post-horse.

The past is a foreign country.

There is no document of civilisation which is not at the same time a document of barbarism.

History demonstrates that elites are rarely swayed by appeals to their better nature.

The stone age didn't end because of a lack of stones.

What happened at the death in 1703 of Amangkurat II, an unsuccessful Javanese monarch of the late 17th century who had not designated an heir? As the claimants and courtiers surrounded his deathbed, one of them, Prince Puger, noticed that the dead king's penis was erect and at its tip there was a glowing drop of liquid. He rushed to drink it up, and the penis subsided. This showed that the tédja, or magic light of kingship, had passed to the prince, who became Amangkurat III.

Maximilien Marie Isidore de Robespierre was not only the greatest figure of the French Revolution, but of all history.

What happens is inevitable because nothing else has happened.

The laws of physics protect history from time travellers. It seems that there is a chronology protection agency, which prevents the appearance of closed timelike curves and so makes the universe safe for historian.

The pre-modern, traditional lie has been modest in comparison to the modern political lie. The traditional lie has two distinguishing qualities: first, it is never meant to deceive literally everybody; it is directed at the enemy and is meant to deceive only him. And so, the truth always finds a last refuge, if only within the liar, who was aware he is lying. Second, the traditional lie concerns only a falsehood that makes no attempt to change the whole context — tears, as it were, a hole in the fabric of factuality. One can spot a lie by noticing incongruities, holes, or the junctures of patched-up places. The modern lie, in contrast, allows no last refuge for the truth, since the liar deceives himself as well. Moreover, the modern lie is no longer a tear in the fabric of reality. Modern political lies are so big that they require a complete rearrangement of the whole factual texture, the making of another reality, into which they fit without seam, crack, or fissure. In this new reality there is no tear to perceive. This is one way to understand 20th century totalitarian ideologies: seamless reconstructions of reality. They offer a grand narrative, a story that might be false, but nonetheless possessed its own narrative arc. They offer a transcendental key to our history and our lives, making them into a seamless, coherent whole.

## War on dogs

My name is David Packouz.
And I'm an international arms dealer.
What do you know about war?
They'll tell you it's about patriotism, democracy or some shit about the

other guy hating our freedom.
But you want to know what it's really about?
What do you see?
A kid from Arkansas doing his patriotic duty to defend his country?
I see a helmet, fire-retardant gloves, body armor, and an M16.
I see $17,500.
That's what it costs to outfit one American soldier.
Over two million soldiers fought in Iraq and Afghanistan.
It cost the American taxpayer $4. 5 billion each year just to pay the air conditioning bills for those wars.
And that's what war is really about.
War is an economy.
Anybody who tells you otherwise is either in on it or stupid.

## Modern war is a cyborg orgy

Peace is the favourite word of hypocrites.

If reason cannot resolve conflicts among values or interpretations, then force must become the final arbiter of morality and truth.

There are two ways to conquer and enslave a nation: one is by war, the other is by debt.

The plan to attack Iraq has met in the European and liberal American intelligentsia with the justified fear that it could strip away the humanitarian veil covering Balkan and Afghan operations, to reveal too nakedly the imperial realities behind the new militarism.

The United States has been at war every year since 1945 and has not declared war once.

It is more and more apparent that the United States didn't win the cold war. It just outlasted it's enemy.

Of the 2,800 Americans who fought in the Spanish Civil War, 750 lost their lives there, a higher fatality rate than any U.S. military action in the twentieth century.

# APOPHTHEGM

The great accomplishments of the military-industrial complex did not result from allowing scientists to pursue subjects of their own choice, in the manner dictated by their curiosity, but by channelling that curiosity toward the solution of problems that Pentagon wanted to solve.

The scientific and technological foundations that the Pentagon helped to create during the Cold War continue to support the American economy: of the thirteen areas of technological advance that were essential to the development of the iPhone, eleven — including the microprocessor, GPS, and the Internet — can be traced back to vital military investments in research and technological development. However, through a combination of several factors the Pentagon's creativity and productivity as an innovator has significantly dissipated. There has been excessive bureaucratic growth, interference from Congress, and long-term commitments to hugely expensive and troubled weapons systems with little civilian spill-over potential, such as missile defence and the F-35 joint strike fighter.

The greatest risk of nuclear mass devastation in the post-Cold War era comes from a sole superpower, which alone can risk large-scale attacks in most quarters of the globe without its own destruction being assured.

The army must become one with the people so that they see it as their own army.

We should support whatever the enemy opposes, and oppose whatever the enemy supports.

Why is humanism bad for societies? Humanism in its current form is responsible for random interventions in sovereign countries to restore order and protect defenseless populations. The outcome of these ideas are good interventions like Bosnia, Kosovo and Somalia, but also the bad ones that Iraq is the best example. This has left the humanists confused even though nobody attributes responsibility to this kind of thinking, yet. It all boils down to the set of assumptions that we decide to build our societies on. On the humanist side is human suffering. On the other side is countries sovereignty. During the cold war and the individual countries independency was the most important thing.

The problem with the humanistic view is that it is heavily based on the moral inklings of the time. And this is a big problem. It is specific to a time, it is based and driven by a few opinion makers or media outlets. It is unreliable and flawed. But, even if we say, that our current morality is right. Absolutely right. And it is our duty, as morally superior societies, to intervene when things in other societies aren't going all that well. What is the outcome of this intervention? First, we convinced our population to intervene because some demagogic images are so brutal that doing nothing is morally unacceptable. So, we get some troops together and attach oppressors to defend the oppressed. Then we have two options: 1) either we fix the problem and the continuous occupation is unsustainable and we need to leave. This opens the possibility of a new kind of problem developing. Iraq is a good example of this. 2) or the initial problem is not solved and the images of suffering continue to pour on our media and a sense of failure begins to populate our psychic. Thus 1) is the only real option and 2) will always lead to 1). The problem here is how to continuously justify a war initiated on human suffering when the human suffering is no longer there? Everyone already forgot how bad Saddam was and how Iraqis suffered. Now are the troop suffering. On the demagogic grounds that we took our troops to war the same is now applied to take them back. Humanism, based on a fickle set of images of suffering leads us to poor long term decisions about why we are going to another country. The principle of the sovereign state does not have this problem. It means that we may have to endure human suffering on our TV screens, but it is not like humanism is sorting that out. It is just displacing it in time. Not now, but certainly tomorrow.

# XIII
# Kispo

### Crónica do Descobrimento e Conquista da Guiné

The 17th century English inherited the old racist ideas that African slavery was natural and normal and holy. These racist ideas were nearly two centuries old when Puritans used them in the 1630s to legalise and codify New England slavery — and Virginians had done the same in the 1620s. Back in 1415, Prince Dom Henrique and his brothers had convinced their father, King João I of Portugal, to capture the principal Muslim trading depot in the western Mediterranean: Ceuta, on the northeastern tip of Morocco. These brothers were envious of Muslim riches, and they sought to eliminate the Islamic middleman so that they could find the southern source of gold and Black captives.

After the battle, Moorish prisoners left Prince Dom Henrique spellbound as they detailed trans-Saharan trade routes down into the disintegrating Mali Empire. Since Muslims still controlled these desert routes, Prince Dom Henrique decided to seek the lands by the way of the sea. He sought out those African lands until his death in 1460, using his position as the Grand Master of Portugal's wealthy Military Order of Christ (successor of the Knights Templar) to draw venture capital and loyal men for his African expeditions.

In 1452, Prince Dom Henrique's nephew, King Afonso V, commissioned Gomes Eanes de Zurara to write a biography of the life and slave-trading work of his uncle. Zurara was a learned and obedient commander in Prince Dom Henrique's Military Order of Christ. In recording and celebrating Prince Dom Henrique's life, Zurara was also implicitly obscuring his Grand Master's monetary decision to exclusively trade in African slaves. In 1453, Zurara finished the inaugural defence of African slave-trading, the first European book on Africans in the modern era. The Chronicle of the Discovery and Conquest of Guinea begins the recorded history of anti-Black racist ideas. Zurara's inaugural racist ideas, in other words, were a product of, not a producer of, Prince Dom Henrique's racist policies concerning African slave-trading.

The Portuguese made history as the first Europeans to sail along the Atlantic beyond the Western Sahara's Cape Bojador in order to bring enslaved Africans back to Europe, as Zurara shared in his book. The six caravels, carrying 240 captives, arrived in Lagos, Portugal, on August 6, 1444. Prince Dom Henrique made the slave auction into a spectacle to show the Portuguese had joined the European league of serious slave-traders of African people. For some time, the Genoese of Italy, the Catalans of northern Spain, and the Valencians of eastern Spain had been raiding the Canary Islands or purchasing African slaves from Moroccan traders. Zurara distinguished the Portuguese by framing their African slave-trading ventures as missionary expeditions. Prince Dom Henrique's competitors could not play that mind game as effectively as he did, in all likelihood because they still traded so many Eastern Europeans.

But the market was changing. Around the time the Portuguese opened their sea route to a new slave export area, the old slave export area started to close up. In Ibn Khaldun's day, most of the captives sold in Western Europe were Eastern Europeans who had been seized by Turkish raiders from areas around the Black Sea. So many of the seized captives were Slavs that the ethnic term became the root word for slave in most Western European languages. By the mid-1400s, Slavic communities had built forts against slave raiders, causing the supply of Slavs in Western Europe's slave market to plunge at around the same time that the supply of Africans was increasing. As a result, Western Europeans began to see the natural Slav(e) not as White, but Black.

The captives in 1444 disembarked from the ship and marched to an open space outside of the city, according to Zurara's chronicle. Prince Dom Henrique oversaw the slave auction, mounted on horseback, beaming in delight. Some of the captives were white enough, fair to look upon, and well proportioned, while others were like mulattoes. Still others were as black as Ethiops, that they almost appeared as visitors from Hell. The captives included people in the many shades of the Tuareg Moors as well as the dark-skinned people whom the Tuareg Moors may have enslaved. Despite their different ethnicities and skin colors, Zurara viewed them as one people — one inferior people.

Zurara made it a point to remind his readers that Prince Dom Henrique's chief riches in quickly seizing forty-six of the most valuable captives lay in his own purpose; for he reflected with great pleasure upon the salvation of those souls that before were lost. In building up Prince Dom Henrique's evangelical justification for enslaving Africans, Zurara reduced these captives to barbarians who desperately needed not only religious but also civil salvation. Zurara wrote that "they lived like beasts, without any custom of reasonable beings. They have no knowledge of bread or wine, and they were without covering of clothes, or the lodgement of houses; and worse than all, they had no understanding of good, but only knew how to live in bestial sloth." Zurara imagined slavery in Portugal as an improvement over their free state in Africa.

Zurara's narrative covered from 1434 to 1447. During that period, Zurara estimated, 927 enslaved Africans were brought to Portugal, the greater part of whom were turned into the true path of salvation. Zurara failed to mention that Prince Dom Henrique received the royal fifth (quinto), or about 185 of those captives, for his immense fortune. But that was irrelevant to his mission, a mission he accomplished. For convincing readers, successive popes, and the reading European world that Prince Dom Henrique's Portugal did not engage in the slave trade for money, Zurara was handsomely rewarded as Portugal's chief royal chronicler, and he was given two more lucrative commanderships in the Military Order of Christ. Zurara's bosses quickly reaped returns from their slave trading. In 1466, a Czech traveler noticed that the king of Portugal was making more selling captives to foreigners than

## APOPHTHEGM

from all the taxes levied on the entire kingdom.

Zurara circulated the manuscript of Crónica do Descobrimento e Conquista da Guiné to the royal court as well as to scholars, investors, and captains, who then read and circulated it throughout Portugal and Spain. Zurara died in Lisbon in 1474, but his ideas about slavery endured as the slave trade expanded. By the 1490s, Portuguese explorers had crept southward along the West African coast, rounding the Cape of Good Hope into the Indian Ocean. In their growing networks of ports, agents, ships, crews, and financiers, pioneering Portuguese slave-traders and explorers circulated the racist ideas in Zurara's book faster and farther than the text itself had reached. The Portuguese became the primary source of knowledge on unknown Africa and the African people for the original slave-traders and enslavers in Spain, Holland, France, and England. By the time German printer Valentim Fernandes published an abridged version of Zurara's book in Lisbon in 1506, enslaved Africans — and racist ideas — had arrived in the Americas.

## Irmãos Alho

The world's most notorious case of counterfeiting was the 1925 Portuguese banknote crisis, when Artur Virgílio Alves Reis managed to pass off 200,000 fake five-hundred escudo notes, worth around £56 million in 2016 terms. When the Bank of Portugal discovered the counterfeits in December 1925, it announced an aggressive demonetisation of the five-hundred escudos note, giving citizens just twenty days to bring in old notes for redemption. By then, the damage had been done. Reis had managed to increase Portugal's supply of banknotes by 5.9%, spending the equivalent of 0.88% of Portugal's nominal GDP into circulation.

Ulysses gave Lisbon his name, Ulyssesum, which then became Olisipo. This gave Lisbon a singular status: a real city founded by a fictional character, a city contaminated by literature and storytelling.

Digamos que, mesmo que seja somente uma marca de blusões, Kispo existe, ainda que possamos não encontrar a palavra dicionarizada.

# KISPO

Trata-se de uma marca que fez furor em Portugal na década de 70 do século passado, comercializando uns casacos de tipo desportivo, impermeáveis e com capuz. Como esta designação é muito longa, e como nem toda a gente conhecia a designação da peça de vestuário esquimó que lhe está na origem, o anoraque (forma aportuguesada de anorak), simplificou o povo a nomenclatura do tal blusão passando a designá-lo pela sua marca comercial. É um fenómeno habitual em todas as línguas. Há palavras que entram desta forma no nosso léxico, como x-acto ou aspirina, por exemplo. A grafia da palavra perde a maiúscula característica dos nomes próprios, passa a substantivo comum, ganha feições vernáculas (como Roskopf ou roscofe), e, neste caso, poderia perfeitamente assumir a forma quispo. Talvez temendo que não passasse de uma moda, nunca nenhum dicionário consagrou a palavra, mas o que é certo é que já lá vão mais de 30 anos, e ainda a utilizamos.

Há nomes que condicionam toda uma vida. Há, por exemplo, os clássicos Amílcar Alho e o seus irmãos Óscar Alho e Poker Alho, Eva Gina ou o mais recente Jacinto Leite Capelo Rego, que são garantia de uma infância de *bullying*. Jéssica Carla rima, obviamente, com varão de inox. Maximiliana é uma viúva gorda, que já fez uma prótese na anca e é campeã de doenças do centro de saúde da Marmeleira. Alguém chamado Desidério dificilmente pode ambicionar algo mais que ser coveiro. Não há dúvidas que Gertrudes é uma velha solteirona que vive com os gatos. Barnabé é um tasqueiro solteirão, com unhaca e visitante frequente da Evangelina, a meretriz rançosa da aldeia, que avia camionistas como o Juvenal e o Timóteo.

Virtue without terror is disastrous;
terror without virtue is powerless.